"Just eighteen minutes a day—what a concept. Dr. Robert Jeffress lays out a plan anyone can follow as he breaks open the ageless lessons of perhaps Christ's greatest sermon. Dr. Jeffress is not someone who wastes words, and page after page of this book is packed full of powerful thoughts and revelations that will change your life."

Jentezen Franklin, senior pastor of Free Chapel and *New York Times* bestselling author

"In this new volume from the prolific pen of Robert Jeffress, in his own unique convincing and convicting style, he reveals that this most famous of all sermons is not just an offering of lengthy, lofty platitudes but is most applicable for every aspect of our daily lives. While you may be able to read the Sermon on the Mount in eighteen minutes, it takes a lifetime to incarnate all its truths. Read it . . . and reap!"

O. S. Hawkins, PhD, former pastor of First Baptist Church, Dallas, and author of the bestselling Code series

"In an ever-changing world and culture, Dr. Jeffress unpacks for us the never-changing words of Jesus. If you long to finish well, dive into these powerful truths."

Sheila Walsh, cohost of *LIFE Today* and author of *Holding On When You Want to Let Go*

"This an important resource for anyone who is ready to have their perspective shifted and their heart challenged, and to experience the fullness of God's kingdom at work in and through their life here on earth. Your spirit will come to a great understanding of how Jesus intended the Sermon on the Mount to impact your life. This book is not just another teaching but a radical invitation to step into all God has destined you to be."

Debbie Lindell, founder of Designed for Life Women's
Conference and author of *She Prays*

"My good friend Robert Jeffress unpacks ten key truths found in one of the most profound messages ever delivered: Jesus's Sermon on the Mount. While this famous sermon takes only eighteen minutes to read, it delivers a life-changing message that transcends time and culture. Jesus is calling us to be revolutionaries, and Jeffress effectively challenges us to allow Christ's words to penetrate our hearts and to live with kingdom purpose."

James Robison, founder and president,
LIFE Outreach International

MINUTES
WITH
JESUS

18 MINUTES WITH JESUS

Straight Talk from the Savior about the Things That Matter Most

DR. ROBERT JEFFRESS

BakerBooks

a division of Baker Publishing Group
Grand Rapids, Michigan

Published by Baker Books
a division of Baker Publishing Group
PO Box 6287, Grand Rapids, MI 49516-6287
www.bakerbooks.com

Printed in the United States of America

Library of Congress Cataloging-in-Publication Data
Names: Jeffress, Robert, 1955– author.
Title: 18 minutes with Jesus : straight talk from the Savior about the things that matter most / Dr. Robert Jeffress.
Other titles: Eighteen minutes with Jesus
Description: Grand Rapids, MI : Baker Books, a division of Baker Publishing Group, [2022] | Includes bibliographical references.
Identifiers: LCCN 2021055596 | ISBN 9781540900487 (cloth) | ISBN 9781493437726 (ebook)
Subjects: LCSH: Sermon on the mount—Criticism, interpretation, etc.
Classification: LCC BT380.3 .J44 2022 | DDC 226.9/06—dc23/eng/20220120
LC record available at https://lccn.loc.gov/2021055596

Published in association with Yates & Yates, www.yates2.com.

Baker Publishing Group publications use paper produced from sustainable forestry practices and post-consumer waste whenever possible.

22   23   24   25   26   27   28   7   6   5   4   3   2   1

To Jeff and Michelle Murphy

Thank you for being faithful partners
in our Pathway to Victory ministry.
I am grateful for your commitment to be
"salt" and "light" in a decaying and darkening
world as we partner together to share the
good news of Jesus Christ.

CONTENTS

ACKNOWLEDGMENTS

In His Sermon on the Mount, Jesus gave us straight talk about the things that matter most—including our relationships. I'm eternally grateful for all the wonderful people God has put in my life. And I've been especially blessed by the talented team God has given me, which includes:

Brian Vos, Mark Rice, Brianna DeWitt, Lindsey Spoolstra, and the whole team at Baker Books, the best publishing partner I've ever worked with.

Derrick G. Jeter, creative director of Pathway to Victory, and Jennifer Stair, who diligently assisted in crafting and polishing the message of this book.

Sealy Yates, my literary agent and friend for more than two decades, who provides wise counsel and consistent encouragement.

Carrilyn Baker, my extraordinary executive associate, who expertly oversees the complicated work of our office with a joyful attitude. And thank you, Mary Shafer, for assisting Carrilyn and me in innumerable ways!

Ben Lovvorn, executive pastor of First Baptist Church, Dallas, and Nate Curtis, Patrick Heatherington, Ben Bugg, and the entire Pathway to Victory team, who extend the message of this book to millions of people around the world.

I'm deeply grateful for the support I receive every day from my family. God has blessed me with two wonderful daughters, Julia and Dorothy, a great son-in-law, Ryan Sadler, and my beloved triplet grandchildren, Barrett, Blake, and Blair.

And at the very top of the list of people in my life for whom I am most grateful is my wife, Amy. Thank you for your consistent encouragement and unconditional love. You are God's greatest blessing of goodness and grace.

18 MINUTES THAT WILL CHANGE YOUR LIFE

IT HAD BEEN A LONG BUT PRODUCTIVE DAY of meetings and ministry at the church I serve as senior pastor. After winding my way home through bumper-to-bumper Dallas traffic, I was grateful to pull up a chair at our kitchen table with my wife, Amy, and enjoy a homemade meal. Then, with a full stomach and contented heart, I settled into my recliner, propped up my feet, and began scrolling through my unread texts.

One message that caught my eye was from a friend. He sent me the link to a video he described as one of the most insightful messages on leadership he had ever heard. Knowing that I enjoy leadership books and podcasts, my friend suggested I watch the video—after all, he pointed out, it was only eighteen minutes long. I wondered, *How could such a short speech make that big an impression?* Then I watched it. My friend was right; even though the video was only eighteen minutes, the speaker had a lot to say.

When delivering a speech or sermon, most people believe longer messages are more persuasive. They have a sort of "longer is stronger" mentality. But that's rarely the case. The truth is, shorter speeches can be far more impactful than longer ones.

I can think of several examples from history to prove my point. When Nathan confronted David after his adultery with Bathsheba and the murder of Uriah, it took the prophet only two minutes to deliver God's message to the king. The result? David repented of his sin.

Abraham Lincoln gave his Gettysburg Address in less than three minutes. Yet today, we remember his speech and not the keynote address delivered that day by Edward Everett, which was two hours long.

And then there's Winston Churchill's famous "Never Give In" speech, which he gave during World War II. It roused a nation to stand firm and fight on—and was delivered in less than twenty minutes.

To this list of short but powerful messages, I would add Jesus's famous Sermon on the Mount. Like the leadership video I watched online, Jesus's hillside sermon is only eighteen minutes long, but it has all the aspects of a successful speech. It is:

- *Short*—you can listen to or read it in eighteen minutes.
- *Informative*—it's filled with practical and sound advice.
- *Original*—it's surprising and contrary to popular opinion.

- *Engaging*—it's witty and interesting.
- *Accessible*—it's free to anyone who cares to listen to or read it.
- *Globally appealing*—its truth transcends time and cultures.

I have no doubt that the men and women who gathered on that grassy hill in Galilee to listen to Jesus's talk that day were shocked by some of the outlandish things He said. His insights about the kingdom of God turned everything they thought they knew about religion upside down. As we'll see, the Sermon on the Mount may be brief, but it goes straight to the heart of the things that matter most.

Straight Talk about the Sermon on the Mount

Before jumping into the nitty-gritty of Jesus's talk, let's get our bearings on the setting of the sermon and Jesus's intended audience. Then we'll look at an important question: Does this message apply to you and me today?

What Was the Setting of the Sermon?

In Matthew's account, the Sermon on the Mount was the first major event in Jesus's ministry, following on the heels of His baptism (3:13–17), His temptation by Satan in the wilderness (4:1–11), and His calling of the Twelve (4:18–22).

Matthew 4:23–24 sets the scene for this sermon: "Jesus was going throughout all Galilee, teaching in their synagogues and proclaiming the gospel of the kingdom, and healing every kind of disease and every kind of sickness among the people. The news about Him spread."

Matthew made it clear that the presenter of this message was not some flash-in-the-pan newcomer but someone who had established Himself as a respected teacher worthy of following. And what a following He had!

Who Was the Intended Audience for the Sermon?

Both Matthew and Luke noted that Jesus was teaching "His disciples" (Matt. 5:1–2; Luke 6:20). In Jesus's day, a disciple ("learner") was somebody who followed a rabbi ("teacher"). To be a disciple meant you were so enthralled with your chosen rabbi that you sought to imitate not just his words but also his example.

So to be a disciple of Jesus means seeking to model your attitudes, actions, and affections after Jesus. It means loving what Jesus loved, acting like Jesus acted, and thinking like Jesus thought in every situation. How would Jesus operate if He had your job? How would Jesus relate to your family and friends? How would Jesus handle the money He entrusted to you? That's what it means to be a disciple of Jesus.

The Gospels record that out of Jesus's many disciples, He chose twelve apostles. The word *apostle* means "one sent forth," similar to an ambassador. Luke 6:12–13 says, "He spent the whole night in prayer to God. And when day came, He called His disciples to Him and chose twelve of them, whom He also named as apostles." These twelve young men were chosen by Jesus to be sent forth on a special assignment to proclaim the gospel. The Bible sometimes refers to the twelve apostles as "His disciples." But during His ministry on earth, Jesus had perhaps hundreds of disciples—men and women who followed Him and His teachings.

Matthew and Luke also described a large crowd that gathered to hear Jesus speak (Matt. 5:1; Luke 6:17–18). This doesn't mean everyone in the crowd was a follower of Jesus. Luke 6:17 clarifies the distinctions between the twelve apostles, the crowd of disciples, and the throng of hangers-on: "Jesus came down with them [*the Twelve*] and stood on a level place; and there was *a large crowd of His disciples*, and *a great throng of people* from all Judea and Jerusalem and the coastal region of Tyre and Sidon."

So, with that background, let's look at Matthew 5:1–2:

> When Jesus saw the crowds, He went up on the mountain; and after He sat down, *His disciples* came to Him. He opened His mouth and began to teach *them*.

Matthew said Jesus was teaching all His followers.[1] In this sermon, He gave us instructions about how to live.

Does the Sermon on the Mount Apply to Us Today?

"Pastor, that's interesting background," you may be saying, "but Jesus gave this talk more than two thousand years ago. Things are very different today. Does His sermon have anything to do with the things that matter to me right now?" Throughout the ages, people have gone to one of two extremes in answering that question about the Sermon on the Mount.

Some people say this sermon applies to us today, but only as a list of requirements of what we must do to go to heaven. If that were true, then Jesus would be no better than the Pharisees, who came up with a long list of rules besides the ones listed in Scripture. Jesus criticized the Pharisees of His day, saying, "They tie up heavy burdens and lay them on men's shoulders" (Matt. 23:4). I don't think that's what Jesus intended in this sermon. Remember, Jesus gave this message to His disciples. This was not a message for the unsaved; this was a message for the saved.

However, other people go to the opposite extreme with the Sermon on the Mount. They agree it is a message for Jesus's followers, but they say these words have no application for our world today. They see this sermon as the constitution for the future millennial kingdom, when Christ will return to set up His rule here on earth.

Is that what Jesus was saying? As I read His words in Matthew 5–7, there is nothing to suggest that this message is for a future generation. In fact, some of these commands would make no sense during the millennium. Turn the other cheek? Pray for those who persecute you? We won't be slapping one another or experiencing persecution in the millennial kingdom. No, this message isn't for the future; it's for now. In this sermon, Jesus was talking about how you and I are to act as Christians today.

Preview of Coming Attractions in the Sermon on the Mount

When I'm getting ready to deliver a new sermon series at First Baptist Church of Dallas, our staff sometimes prepares a short video—much like a movie trailer—to whet the congregation's appetite for what's ahead. I want to do the same for you here.

There are many ways to outline the Sermon on the Mount. In this book, I've divided the key topics of Jesus's talk into ten chapters, each focused on an issue that matters to us today.

Straight Talk about Your Happiness

Jesus began His talk by describing eight attitudes that will lead us to a joy-filled life. This passage (Matt. 5:3–12), called the Beatitudes, includes some of the most familiar verses in the Bible, but they're also some of the most misunderstood. What does it really mean to be blessed? If we want to experience true and lasting joy, then we must grasp what Jesus meant when He said, "Blessed are . . ."

Straight Talk about Your Faith

Christians are called to be salt and light—living out our faith in such a way that we cause others to thirst for God. The instructions on how to do that are found in the Word of God. It's a manual, so to speak, for living faithful and righteous lives. And since Jesus is the author of the Bible, we ought to understand what He thought about it and learn how to read it correctly (vv. 13–20).

Straight Talk about Your Relationships

When it comes to the subject of murder, we tend to think literally—about the physical taking of another's life. So did Jesus's original listeners. But Jesus meant more than the literal killing of another; He drove to the heart of the matter—hatred—and challenged us to examine our own hearts when anger gets the best of us (vv. 21–26).

Straight Talk about Your Sex Life

Like we do with murder, we tend to think of adultery in a literal sense: having sex with somebody who is not your spouse. But adultery doesn't begin in the bedroom; it begins in our hearts and minds (vv. 27–30). So we need to gain control of our minds before we lose control of our bodies, which too often leads to broken marriages. How can we do this? We can start by looking at what Jesus said about adultery (vv. 31–32).

Straight Talk about Your Adversaries

If we're honest, all of us have savored the thought of retaliating against someone who has hurt us. And in our age of social media, it's easy to get revenge by spreading lies and slander. Many of us have done just that. But Jesus offered a better way. Instead of seeking vengeance and holding grudges, let us learn to love and pray for those who've hurt us (vv. 38–48).

Straight Talk about Your Church

In Matthew 6, Jesus transitioned from how believers are to treat other people to how we are to practice our faith. He began with the practice of giving offerings in church and the attitude behind our giving—whether to please God or to please others. If we seek to please God, then we have a divine reward waiting for us. But if we seek to please others, then we have already received our reward (vv. 1–4).

Straight Talk about Your Prayer Life

Of all the practices in the Christian life, praying is one of the most fundamental—and one of the most difficult. But it ought not to be. In the Lord's Prayer (which should really be called the Disciples' Prayer), Jesus provided a master class on how to speak to the Father. This prayer's simplicity and straightforwardness are a model for all of us to follow (vv. 5–15).

Straight Talk about Your Money

Wealth (or the lack thereof) and worry go hand in hand, like apple pie and vanilla ice cream. Of all the things that hinder followers of Christ from giving and praying for God's will, perhaps the most crippling is our anxiety over money—worrying whether we have enough or how we can get a little bit more. We desperately need to listen to what Jesus had to say about wealth and put it in its proper place in our lives (vv. 19–34).

Straight Talk about Your Needs

God created humans to be independent but also *interdependent*. We depend on any number of things to keep us alive and to help us flourish. Simply put, we have needs. And many of those needs cannot be fulfilled by others or within ourselves; only God can fulfill them. But it can be scary relying on God alone, so what did Jesus have to say about that? Plenty. We'll explore what He said in Matthew 7:7–12.

Straight Talk about Your Eternal Destiny

One of the greatest fears people have is of the future. Is there really a heaven and a hell? And if there is, how can we be sure where we'll spend eternity? We'll see how Jesus answered these questions in Matthew 7:13–27. His answers are just as applicable today as they were two thousand years ago.

Jesus's Call to Radical Righteousness

Few sections of Scripture force us to take a hard look into our hearts as does the Sermon on the Mount. But attaining the righteousness Jesus spoke of in this sermon is more than just coming to faith in Christ. The moment we place our trust in Jesus, He sends the Holy Spirit to take up residence in our lives and help us live out the righteousness Jesus calls us to.

Paul wrote in Galatians 5:16, "Walk by the Spirit, and you will not carry out the desire of the flesh." We are to rely on the Spirit day by day, hour by hour, to control our thoughts, our emotions, our attitudes, and our actions. When we do, Paul said, "[We] can do all things through Him who strengthens [us]" (Phil. 4:13). Jesus Christ not only calls us to a life of righteousness in Matthew 5–7 but also empowers us to attain such righteousness.

Jesus was revolutionary—then and now. And what we call the Sermon on the Mount is one of the best examples of just how radical Jesus really was (and is). In this brief but powerful message, Jesus went straight to the heart of the things that matter most.

If we are going to be the people Jesus has called us to be, then we need to live as He has called us to live and experience the blessings He wants us to enjoy—not just in some future kingdom but *now*! If that sounds like something you'd like to do, then let's look at Jesus's eighteen-minute message. It will change your life.

Straight Talk about Your Happiness

THOSE OF US WHO ARE PARENTS have mental snapshots of our children—particularly memorable scenes from their lives we will never forget. For my younger daughter, Dorothy, one of my snapshots comes from her senior year in high school, when she was standing on a stage in a blue-and-white checked dress singing "Somewhere over the Rainbow" as the lead character Dorothy in the musical *The Wizard of Oz.*

Chances are you know the story of Dorothy and her dog, Toto, who were caught up in a tornado and transported to the Land of Oz. You probably know the story from the 1939 film starring Judy Garland, not L. Frank Baum's children's book. The film gets many of the book's details correct: Dorothy wants to return home to Kansas and travels the Yellow

Brick Road to the Emerald City to ask for the wizard's help. Her traveling companions include the Scarecrow, who wants a brain; the Cowardly Lion, who wants courage; and the Tin Man, who wants a heart.

The book explains why the Tin Man wants a heart. After being rescued from his rust-encrusted prison, the Tin Man tells Dorothy and the Scarecrow the sad tale of how he turned to tin and lost his ability to love. "It was a terrible thing to undergo," he said, "but during the year I stood there I had time to think that the greatest loss I had known was the loss of my heart. While I was in love I was the happiest man on earth; but no one can love who has not a heart, and so I am resolved to ask Oz to give me one."

Scarecrow said, "I shall ask for brains instead of a heart; for a fool would not know what to do with a heart if he had one."

But the Tin Man had a different perspective. "I shall take the heart," he insisted, "for brains do not make one happy, and happiness is the best thing in the world."[1]

That sounds right, but is it *really* true? Is happiness truly the "best thing in the world"?

The word *happiness* comes from the Old English word *hap*, meaning "chance" or "luck." I think of it like this: *Happiness happens when what happens is something we want to happen.* For example, I'm happy when I'm sitting on the sofa with my wife, Amy, enjoying a bowl of vanilla Häagen-Dazs ice cream after dinner. But I'm definitely unhappy when I spy an empty ice-cream carton in the trash can!

Jesus got to the heart of whether happiness is the best thing in the world at the beginning of His hillside sermon, in the section of His talk we know as the Beatitudes.

The Blessed Attitudes

The Beatitudes (from the Latin *beatus*, meaning "blessed") are eight attitudes that reflect the character of all true followers of Jesus Christ. Each beatitude includes a reward that will be fulfilled when Jesus Christ returns and establishes His kingdom on the earth. But until that day comes, we who follow Him are to be characterized by these eight attitudes.

Before we look at each one, let's consider what Jesus meant when He used the term *blessed*. Now, *blessed* is one of those Christianese words we use, often with little understanding of what we are saying. Have you ever noticed people who suffer from a severe case of "blessitis" in their public prayers? ("Bless the pastor," "bless the missionaries," "bless the church," and "bless anyone who will ever sneeze!") To ask for someone to be blessed sounds good, but what does it really mean?

Blessed: The Approval of God

The Greek word *makarios*, or "blessed," doesn't have a precise English equivalent, but it's akin to joy—an inner contentment that is unshakable. It's a joy that never falters and can never be taken away, just as Jesus promised: "No one will take your joy away from you" (John 16:22). As we have seen, happiness is a superficial emotion that depends on happenings, or circumstances. But joy is a deep, bedrock assurance that God is in control of the happenings of our lives and is using them for our good and His glory.

"Wait a minute, Pastor," you may be saying. "My life is full of difficult circumstances and difficult people. How can I have unshakable joy?" That's what the Sermon on the Mount is all about. When you see the big picture of the coming kingdom of God, you can be joyful no matter what circumstances you face.

More than that, those who are blessed are overcome with joy because they have found favor with God. When God blesses us, He approves of us. What could be greater than that? As Max Lucado so beautifully titled his book on the Beatitudes, blessedness is knowing you have "the applause of heaven."[2]

Though many people today adopt the Tin Man's philosophy of life, believing happiness is the best thing in the world, Jesus had a different philosophy. In this sermon, He showed us that the greatest thing in the world is God's approval and the lasting joy that accompanies it. And the Beatitudes are the key to unlocking the blessed life.

The Be-Attitudes

Christianity is more than just what we believe and what we do; it also involves who we are. The Beatitudes show us that it's not enough simply to believe right and do right; we must also *be* right. We must *be* people who reflect the character of Christ. That's what *Christian* means: "little Christ." And that's why the eight character traits listed in Matthew 5:3–10 have been called *be*-attitudes.[3] If we want to receive God's blessing, then we need to reflect the characteristics that bring God's blessing.

The first four Beatitudes focus on our relationship to God, while the second four focus on our relationships with one another. Each builds upon the other, creating a progression:

> Blessed are the poor in spirit, for theirs is the
> kingdom of heaven.
> Blessed are those who mourn, for they shall be
> comforted.

> Blessed are the gentle, for they shall inherit the earth.
> Blessed are those who hunger and thirst for
>   righteousness, for they shall be satisfied.
> Blessed are the merciful, for they shall receive
>   mercy.
> Blessed are the pure in heart, for they shall see God.
> Blessed are the peacemakers, for they shall be called
>   sons of God.
> Blessed are those who have been persecuted for the
>   sake of righteousness, for theirs is the kingdom of
>   heaven. (Matt. 5:3–10)

Though each is distinct, there's a beautiful unity. The first and last beatitudes end with the same reward: "for theirs is the kingdom of heaven" (vv. 3, 10), indicating that the entire list deals with God's kingdom.

The rewards spring supernaturally out of each attitude, requiring us to submit to the Holy Spirit in our lives. When we hunger and thirst for righteousness, for example, God will see that we're filled with righteousness. When we show mercy, we'll receive mercy in return.

The Paradox of the Beatitudes

G. K. Chesterton wrote, "Paradox has been defined as 'Truth standing on her head to attract attention.'"[4] And few things are more paradoxical and attention-grabbing than the Beatitudes. In the Beatitudes, Jesus turned what we think we know about the world on its head and declared this new perspective "blessed." Then He offered a promise with each topsy-turvy saying. The Beatitudes are counterintuitive— truths doing handstands.

The Riches of Poverty

Jesus began His sermon with, "Blessed are the poor in spirit, for theirs is the kingdom of heaven" (Matt. 5:3). Jesus was not talking about material poverty here. He wasn't saying there is something particularly blessed about being financially poor. Being poor doesn't automatically make you more holy. When Jesus said "the poor in spirit," He was talking about those who are impoverished spiritually.

The Greek word translated as "poor" (*ptochos*) means "to cower, cringe, or crouch like a beggar." Applied to spirituality, it characterizes a person who is bankrupt of spiritual resources, which accurately describes each of us. Isaiah put it like this: "We are all infected and impure with sin. When we display our righteous deeds, they are nothing but filthy rags" (Isa. 64:6 NLT). And Paul wrote, "There is none righteous, not even one . . . for all have sinned and fall short of the glory of God" (Rom. 3:10, 23).

In Luke 18, Jesus illustrated what it means to be "poor in spirit." In this parable, two men went to the temple: a Pharisee and a tax collector. The Pharisee prayed, "God, I thank You that I am not like other people: swindlers, unjust, adulterers, or even like this tax collector" (v. 11). However, the tax collector prayed with his head hung low and beat his chest, saying, "God, be merciful to me, the sinner!" (v. 13). That's what it means to be "poor in spirit." The tax collector approached God in a spirit of utter dependence and found the doors of the kingdom flung open. But the doors were slammed shut in the face of the prideful Pharisee.

I like the way author Dallas Willard said it: "Blessed are the spiritual zeros."[5] Have you ever felt like a spiritual zero?

Do you feel like you're not succeeding in your Christian life? You know you ought to pray more and read the Bible more, but you just can't do it, and you wish you could be better than you are? Jesus said, "Be joyful. Because one day that struggle you have in your Christian life is going to be satisfied."

To the poor in spirit, Jesus gave this promise: "Theirs is the kingdom of heaven" (Matt. 5:3). When we come to God with nothing in our hands to offer but our spiritual bankruptcy, He gives us the key to heaven, not only for our salvation today but also for the right to rule in His kingdom tomorrow.

The Comfort of Mourning

In Jesus's second beatitude, He said, "Blessed are those who mourn, for they shall be comforted" (Matt. 5:4). The Greek word for "mourn" (*pentheo*) describes those who feel anguish over a distressing situation, like the death of a loved one.

Losing a loved one through death is painful. Unfortunately, I know that grief all too well—I've mourned the deaths of my parents, as well as many close friends. But I believe something even more painful is losing a loved one through defection. Their heart turns cold toward you. They leave you. Maybe you have suffered the loss of a loved one either through death or defection. Jesus was saying, "Blessed are you who weep right now, for one day you will be comforted."

More than the mourning that accompanies losing someone, Jesus also had in mind those who mourn over their sins. This mourning naturally follows the poverty of spirit. To believe you're "poor in spirit" is an act of the *intellect*, agreeing with God's assessment of who you really are. But to mourn over your failure before God goes much deeper than intellectual agreement about your transgression.

I'm concerned about a particular strain of Christian teaching today that says you can acknowledge your sin without feeling sorry for your sin. No! You will never turn from your sin until you are first of all broken over your sin. To mourn over your sin is an act of the *emotions* as well as the intellect.

This was the case with the apostle Peter. After Peter disowned the Lord three times, "he went out and *wept bitterly*" (Luke 22:62). The apostle Paul was also deeply remorseful for his sins, saying, "Wretched man that I am!" (Rom. 7:24).

Are you grieved over your sin? Do you find yourself, like Peter and Paul, reeling over your own sinfulness? Then this beatitude gives you hope! When you turn to the Lord in your mourning and confess your sins to Him, you will receive God's forgiveness (1 John 1:9), and He will comfort you. In 2 Corinthians 7:10, Paul said, "The sorrow that is according to the will of God produces a repentance without regret, leading to salvation." Godly mourning, or sorrow, for your sin is temporary and leads to repentance.

Mourning over sin is natural, especially when we realize our spiritual poverty. But we're also called to mourn over sin in the lives of others. Paul told the Ephesian elders to remember, "Night and day for a period of three years I did not cease to admonish each one *with tears*" (Acts 20:31). And he wrote to the Philippians, "Many walk, of whom I often told you, and now tell you *even weeping*, that they are enemies of the cross of Christ, whose end is destruction, whose god is their appetite, and whose glory is in their shame, who set their minds on earthly things" (3:18–19).

To those who mourn over sin, Jesus gave this promise: "They shall be comforted" (Matt. 5:4). No one said it better than David after his sin with Bathsheba: "The sacrifices of God are a broken spirit; a broken and a contrite heart, O God, You will not despise" (Ps. 51:17).

The Strength of Meekness

Theodore Roosevelt supposedly said William McKinley "[possessed] no more backbone than a chocolate éclair."[6] That's how we tend to think of those who are described as "meek" or "gentle." We assume they are wimps, doormats, or pushovers.

In reality, meekness isn't weakness at all. It's more akin to Superman-like strength. In classical Greek, the same word was used to describe wild animals that had been tamed. *Meekness* can be defined as "power under control." No wonder Jesus said, "Blessed are the gentle" (Matt. 5:5).

Gentleness is a characteristic close to the Lord's heart. He described Moses as "very meek, above all the men which were upon the face of the earth" (Num. 12:3 KJV). And it's the only characteristic Jesus used to describe Himself. "Come unto Me," He said, "for I am meek and lowly in heart" (Matt. 11:28–29 KJV).

When C. S. Lewis wanted to depict Jesus in his children's series The Chronicles of Narnia, he didn't choose a fluffy bunny; he chose a lion. In one of the most moving scenes in his book *The Lion, the Witch and the Wardrobe*, Mr. and Mrs. Beaver tell the children about Aslan, the King of the wood. Lucy wants to know if Aslan is a man, and Mr. Beaver tells her he's a lion. Susan asks, "Is he—quite safe? I shall feel rather nervous about meeting a lion." Mr. Beaver scoffs at the question. "Safe? Who said anything about safe? 'Course he isn't safe. But he's good. He's the King, I tell you."[7]

And that makes all the difference.

To those who are gentle, or meek, Jesus gave this promise: "They shall inherit the earth" (5:5). David affirmed this promise in Psalm 37:11: "The meek shall inherit the earth; and shall delight themselves in the abundance of peace" (KJV).

What does it mean to "inherit the earth"? As a friend has said, "It doesn't mean there will be a Mercedes in every garage, a mink in every closet, or a million dollars in every bank account. It's a promise of things to come—things that cannot be stolen or destroyed. It's the promise of a new earth, a better earth—an earth without sin—and the right of the meek and gentle to possess it."[8]

The Fullness of Hunger

All of us hunger physically for food and water, and we also hunger spiritually for God. In the Beatitudes, Jesus addressed this spiritual hunger. He said, "Blessed are those who hunger and thirst for righteousness" (Matt. 5:6).

"Righteousness" is often used in the Bible to refer to the act of spiritual justification in which God exchanges our unrighteousness with Christ's righteousness at the moment of faith and declares us "not guilty" (Rom. 4:5; Phil. 3:9; 1 Pet. 3:18). But that's not what Jesus meant here. Jesus was talking about spiritual hunger and thirst for what I call "ethical righteousness," which refers to behavior that aligns with God's commands.

The term *social justice* has become radioactive lately because of the political baggage associated with it. But politics aside, do you ever wish we lived in a world where justice reigns? Do you wish we had a world without terrorist attacks? Do you wish evil would be overcome by good every time? That's what Jesus was talking about when He declared, "Blessed are those who hunger and thirst for righteousness," for one day the tables are going to be turned, and God is going to right the wrongs of this world.

This also applies to the hunger and thirst for righteousness in our own lives. You've heard it said, "You are what you eat"—which makes me one-fourth steak and three-fourths Häagen-Dazs ice cream! What's true physically is equally true spiritually. If you crave violence, materialism, or eroticism, then eventually you'll personify these things. But if you crave righteousness, then you'll personify the fruit of the Spirit outlined in Galatians 5:22–23: "Love, joy, peace, patience, kindness, goodness, faithfulness, gentleness, [and] self-control." That's why Paul advised in Philippians 4:8, "Whatever is true, whatever is honorable, whatever is right, whatever is pure, whatever is lovely, whatever is of good repute, if there is any excellence and if anything worthy of praise, dwell on these things." If you hunger and thirst for righteousness in your own life, then this promise is for you: "They shall be satisfied" (Matt. 5:6).

When we desire to conform to God's will, the Lord satisfies that desire. Then we have a renewed desire for deeper conformity, which the Lord also satisfies—until our spiritual stomachs hunger again and our spiritual throats thirst again. And the cycle continues.

My church employs a professional to cook for special occasions, Chef Tim. He makes a triple chocolate cake that can almost transport you to heaven. One day, someone dropped off a piece of Chef Tim's cake at my office. I told myself, *One bite, and one bite only, Robert.* And when I took that bite, I blissfully leaned back in my chair, satisfied—for about three minutes. Then I hungered for another bite. So I dipped my fork, and again I resolved, *Just this bite, and no more.* But it was *so* good I couldn't help myself. The cycle continued until you couldn't have found a crumb on the plate.

Jesus said those who hunger and thirst for righteousness will be satisfied by a heaping helping of a clear conscience; deeper love of God and others; and freedom from fear, shame, and regret. One day the kingdom of God is coming, and we are going to see His rule. Who isn't hungry for that?

The Mystery of Mercy

For many people, mercy is a mystery, easily confused with grace. The simplest distinction is this: grace is receiving what we *do not* deserve; mercy is *not* receiving what we *do* deserve. Some people see mercy as greater than justice. James hinted at this when he wrote, "Judgment will be merciless to one who has shown no mercy; mercy triumphs over judgment" (2:13). Where justice says, "Punish," mercy says, "Forgive." Where justice says, "Pay the debt," mercy says, "Forgive the debt."

Mercy cuts against our natural inclinations, especially when we're asked to extend it. But Jesus said, "Blessed are the merciful" (Matt. 5:7). In one sense, to show mercy means to pardon those who have wronged us. That is what Joseph did when he said to his brothers after they had wronged him, "Am I in God's place? As for you, you meant evil against me, but God meant it for good in order to bring about this present result, to preserve many people alive. So therefore, do not be afraid; I will provide for you and your little ones" (Gen. 50:19–21).

Mercy is the perfect antidote to the poison of bitterness.

In another sense, mercy means to reach out to those who are hurting or in need. The story is told that after Queen Victoria's husband, Prince Albert, died, she visited a friend who had just lost her own husband. When the queen arrived unannounced, her friend rose and began to curtsy. The queen put up a hand and said, "My dear, don't rise. I am not coming to you today as the queen to a subject, but as one woman who has lost her husband to another."[9]

James wrote, "Pure and undefiled religion in the sight of our God and Father is this: to visit orphans and widows in their distress" (1:27). He also said, "If a brother or sister is without clothing and in need of daily food, and one of you says to them, 'Go in peace, be warmed and be filled,' and yet you do not give them what is necessary for their body, what use is that?" (2:15–16). John answered that question with one of his own: "Whoever has the world's goods, and sees his brother in need and closes his heart against him, how does the love of God abide in him?" (1 John 3:17).

Have you been wronged by somebody? Do you know somebody who could use your help? Mercy is needed in such times. And to give mercy is to receive mercy. That's what Jesus said: "Blessed are the merciful, for they shall receive mercy" (Matt. 5:7). We get what we give. And if we have received the mercy of God through the crucifixion of His beloved Son, then we must be willing to give mercy—and it will return to us in our own time of need.

The Vision of Purity

In Psalm 24:3–4, David asked, "Who may ascend into the hill of the LORD? And who may stand in His holy place? He who has clean hands and a pure heart, who has not lifted up his soul to falsehood and has not sworn deceitfully."

This stands behind Jesus's blessing in Matthew 5:8: "Blessed are the pure in heart, for they shall see God."

In Jesus's day, the Pharisees focused on their external appearance, wanting people to see their best side. (Sounds a little bit like today's obsession with image consultants and Instagram filters, doesn't it?) Later in the Gospel of Matthew, Jesus lowered the boom on these religious leaders by calling them dirty dishes and "whitewashed tombs" (23:27) who were interested only in *appearing* righteous, not actually *being* righteous.

Appearances can be deceiving. For example, people who travel to the mountains may think mountain streams are clean and clear. But take an unfiltered drink, and you'll be sorry you did. The water might look clear, but it's usually filled with unseen parasites. The same is true of those who look righteous on the outside but inside are "full of dead men's bones" (v. 27). Jesus is interested in the heart.

Now, when we think about our hearts, we tend to think about our emotions. But the word for *heart* in the Bible is an umbrella word for the totality of your being. It includes not only your emotions but also your intellect and your will. In the Jewish culture of Jesus's day, your heart was all that you are. And Jesus said the heart God blesses is one that is pure—singularly devoted to God in thoughts, feelings, and actions.

Let me illustrate it this way. The greatest words I can ever say to my wife, Amy, are, "I love you with my whole heart"— and then I show her that love by my attitudes and actions. My inward attitude and outward actions confirm that my love for Amy is undivided, that there's no rival to her. That's what Jesus was getting at when He said, "Blessed are the pure in heart."

Those with sincere, undivided, and pure hearts are blessed, Jesus said, "for they shall see God" (5:8). We see what we want to see. I'm reminded of the story of the psychologist who used the famous Rorschach test to discover what was in his patient's subconscious. "What is the first word that comes to your mind when you see this?" the doctor asked. Yet no matter what inkblot the doctor showed his patient, the patient always answered, "Sex." Finally, the exasperated psychologist said, "You're obsessed with sex!" The patient replied, "What do you mean? *You're* the one drawing all the dirty pictures!"

Those with impure hearts see in every situation nothing but sin, sexual innuendo, and dirty jokes. But those who are pure in heart see the hand of God, whether it's in nature (Ps. 29:3–4, 7–10), in the face of a child (139:13–16), or in the ever-deepening intimacy we experience with Him (1 Cor. 8:3). This is the pure vision that receives the blessing of God.

The Paternity Test of Peace

It's been said, "Peace is that brief glorious moment in history when everybody stands around reloading."[10] But that isn't peace. Peace isn't the absence of hostilities between enemies bent on destroying each other—that's an armistice, like the one that currently exists between North and South Korea. Peace means something is at rest. A rock that has tumbled down a hill and comes to rest is at peace. A cat curled up in a sunny spot on the sofa is at peace. But biblically speaking, peace means much more. The Greek term translated as "peace," *eirene*, is similar in meaning to the Hebrew term *shalom*, conveying the idea of wholeness and overall well-being.

Shalom is a blessing conferred on another. Is it any wonder, then, that in Matthew 5:9, Jesus said, "Blessed are the peacemakers"? The makers of peace—those who actively pursue it—don't simply want others to be free from conflict; they want others to flourish. They make their life verse Hebrews 12:14: "Pursue peace with all men." They seek to relieve tension, not fuel the fires of disagreements. They seek to resolve disputes, not egg on additional controversies. They seek to reconcile fractured relationships, not drive a wedge between people.

This isn't to say that peacemakers are laissez-faire about life, with an attitude that says, "You do you, and I'll do me." They aren't appeasers, willing to make peace at any price. Rather, peacemakers are interested in right living. As James said, "The seed whose fruit is righteousness is sown in peace by those who make peace" (3:18). Instead of waging war, peacemakers "wage peace," pursuing "the things which make for peace and the building up of one another" (Rom. 14:19).

Peacemakers reflect the Prince of Peace, which is why Jesus said, "They shall be called sons of God" (Matt. 5:9). Jesus came to reconcile sinners to a holy God—to make peace between humanity and God. This is what the prophet Isaiah said the Messiah would do: "How lovely on the mountains are the feet of him who brings good news, who *announces peace* and brings good news of happiness, who announces salvation" (52:7).

Following in His footsteps, we proclaim peace whenever we proclaim the gospel, whenever we bring reconciliation to enemies, and whenever we submit to the work of the Holy Spirit in our lives. As peacemakers, we find peace within our own souls and become instruments of peace in the lives of those around us.

Let me get very practical and personal, if I may. Many of us who serve as pastors feel like we should dress for church by putting on a black-and-white referee's shirt because it seems we are constantly working to keep the peace between church members, especially during these volatile times when Christians are ready to divide over any and every issue. If I wanted to, I could divide my church right down the middle over a dozen issues. But whenever I'm tempted to draw a line in the sand over issues that are not biblical imperatives but personal opinions, I remember my mother saying these words to me when I was a little boy trying to make peace between my brother and sister: "Robert, remember, 'Blessed are the peacemakers, for they shall be called the children of God.'"

Making peace—and doing everything we can to "preserve the unity of Spirit in the bond of peace" (Eph. 4:3)—should be the desire of anyone who wants to be known as a child of God. The desire to keep the peace, instead of disrupt the peace, is our true spiritual paternity test.

The Joy of Persecution

If we want to live out the Beatitudes through the power of the Holy Spirit, we have to adopt attitudes and actions that are contrary to our culture. And living in a countercultural way invites the enmity of the world, just as Jesus said: "If you find the godless world is hating you, remember it got its start hating me. If you lived on the world's terms, the world would love you as one of its own. But since I picked you to live on God's terms and no longer on the world's terms, the world is going to hate you" (John 15:18–19 Message). And when it does, Jesus declared, "Blessed are those who have been persecuted for the sake of righteousness" (Matt. 5:10).

Many Christians read this beatitude like this: "Blessed are the persecuted, period!" They believe any and all opposition results in God's applause. But that's not what Jesus was saying here. Sometimes Christians are "persecuted" because they are doing things that are rude, insensitive, or piously obnoxious. In those cases, the Lord doesn't applaud.

Peter clarified the persecution Jesus was talking about in the Beatitudes: "If you are reviled for the name of Christ, you are blessed, because the Spirit of glory and of God rests on you. Make sure that none of you suffers as . . . [an] evil-doer, or a troublesome meddler; but if anyone suffers as a Christian, he is not to be ashamed, but is to glorify God in this name" (1 Pet. 4:14–16). Notice that if you are persecuted "for the name of Christ" and "as a Christian," then, and only then, will you be blessed.

Of course, persecution doesn't always mean imprisonment or execution. I define *persecution* as "any negative consequence you experience for your obedience to God." Persecution comes in all shapes and sizes, and it is usually incremental. Teenagers and young adults, do you ever feel like you're being ostracized from the rest of the group because of your commitment to Christ? Adults, do you feel like you've been passed over for a promotion or even lost your job because you won't bend your Christian principles? Is there a division in your family between you and your mate, your children, or your parents because of your Christian faith? That's all part of the price for living for Christ. But Jesus went on to give the persecuted this blessing: "Theirs is the kingdom of heaven" (v. 10).

Let me illustrate that truth this way. Let's say, like many people, you're just keeping your head above water financially, trying to meet your expenses. Every month, you're hoping you run out of month before you run out of money. You're having a struggle. Money is tight. That's the bad news. The good news is you have an uncle who has left an irrevocable trust for you of $10 million that will be yours when he dies. And the even better news is he's ninety-nine years old. Now, what does that knowledge do for you?

Does the existence of that trust alleviate your day-to-day struggle? No, it doesn't eradicate your money problem, but it does give you a different perspective about it, doesn't it? You know your problem is temporary. There's a great reward coming. And that's what Jesus was saying here. Yes, your difficult circumstances are real and painful, but when you know what Jesus knows about the future, you can be generous in your attitude toward those difficult circumstances.

That's why He said, "Blessed are you when people insult you and persecute you, and falsely say all kinds of evil against you because of Me. Rejoice and be glad, for your reward in heaven is great" (vv. 11–12).

Dare to Be Different

So what do these "be-attitudes" mean for us today? Simple: if you want God to smile on you—if you want His applause— then dare to be different. Buck the system and follow Christ with a whole heart, adopting His attitudes and actions as outlined in the Beatitudes. You'll be the blessed one if you do.

How do you think and act differently from the surrounding culture and make the Beatitudes part of your everyday life? Let me give you a simple exercise to follow: *practice one beatitude every day*. Meditate on one a day, and ask God to help you live it out throughout that day. Here are the eight "be-attitudes" one more time, in case you've forgotten them:

> Blessed are the poor in spirit, for theirs is the kingdom of heaven.
> Blessed are those who mourn, for they shall be comforted.
> Blessed are the gentle, for they shall inherit the earth.
> Blessed are those who hunger and thirst for righteousness, for they shall be satisfied.
> Blessed are the merciful, for they shall receive mercy.
> Blessed are the pure in heart, for they shall see God.
> Blessed are the peacemakers, for they shall be called sons of God.
> Blessed are those who have been persecuted for the sake of righteousness, for theirs is the kingdom of heaven. (Matt. 5:3–10)

Practice one of these attitudes each day for a month. At the end of the month, evaluate your relationship with Christ and how it may have changed. And then continue into the next month . . . and the next . . . and the next.

What will you gain?

Only the blessing of God.

two

Straight Talk about Your Faith

WHEN ABRAHAM LINCOLN was putting together his cabinet, an adviser suggested a certain man. But Lincoln refused, saying, "I don't like the man's face." Taken aback, the adviser said, "But sir, he can't be responsible for his face." Not so, said Lincoln: "Every man . . . is responsible for his own face."[1]

I sometimes think of that line when talking with fellow Christians. Too often, Christ-followers today look like they've been "baptized in lemon juice."[2] Now, don't get me wrong; I'm not saying we should paint on fake smiles and sing "Zip-a-Dee-Doo-Dah" every day. Naturally, there are times when we are mourning a loss or brokenhearted over sin, as Jesus said in the Beatitudes (Matt. 5:3–4), or when we are persecuted because of our commitment to Christ (vv. 10–11).

It's normal to be downcast at such moments—and weird if we're not.

But neither should we be all sour-looking. The apostle Paul wasn't, even when he was confined in prison and chained to a different Roman soldier every eight hours, awaiting trial to see whether he was going to live or die. During those two years in prison, Paul wrote four books of the New Testament: Colossians, Ephesians, Philemon, and Philippians. Do you know what the key word is in his letter to the Philippians? *Joy.* Nineteen times in this short letter, Paul referred to "joy," "rejoicing," or "gladness."

How could Paul be joyful while he was in prison? And how can we, too, have that kind of joy, even during difficult times? Remember, as we saw in the previous chapter, joy isn't the same as happiness. Happiness is a temporary emotion based on our circumstances. But joy is a choice we make. It's a permanent and deep-seated sense of well-being, no matter what comes our way.

The apostle James was getting at this when he wrote, "Consider it all *joy,* my brethren, when you encounter various trials" (1:2), not because trials in and of themselves are joyful but because of what trials can produce in our lives: Christlikeness (vv. 3–4). Peter made the same point about joy when he wrote to believers who were being persecuted for their faith (1 Pet. 1:3–9).

The point is this: What's *inside* of us shows up *outside* of us. Our character, the "be-attitudes" we studied in chapter 1, will be demonstrated in our conduct. In other words, how we live affects our witness to the world.

What does your face say about your faith? Do you look like the cover photo for the book of Lamentations, or does your face exude a winsome attitude? Does your life exhibit the joy you have in Christ, regardless of your circumstances? In the next section of His message we call the Sermon on the Mount, Jesus gave His followers straight talk about how we are to live out our faith in the world.

Shake and Shine

Jesus understood that knowledge by itself changes no one. That's why, when you look at the teachings of Jesus, you'll see that whether it was the Sermon on the Mount or the parables or His discourses about the end times, Jesus related His message to everyday life and showed His audience how to live out that truth. In Matthew 5:13–20, Jesus illustrated His teaching about how Christians are to conduct ourselves in the world by using two common commodities of His day: salt and light.

Jesus said, "You are the salt of the earth" (v. 13) and "You are the light of the world" (v. 14). I want you to notice three things about these key phrases. First of all, these statements are parallel to each other. They are both affirmations, declaring that something positive is true. And they are both confirmations, assuring that something positive will happen.

Second, Jesus emphasized the pronoun "you" by placing it at the beginning of each pronouncement. If you're a basketball fan, you might remember a chant that often echoed in arenas a few years ago whenever the opposing team drew a foul. The crowd would point and yell, "You, you, *you*, YOU, YOU!" Well, Jesus was doing something similar: "You, you, *you*, YOU, YOU are the salt of the earth," he said. "You, you, *you*, YOU, YOU are the light of the world." This doesn't just apply to those who have been to seminary or work in vocational ministry. This reminder is for all believers. To you, reading this book. YOU! Everyone in God's family is to shake and shine. No one is excluded.

Third, Jesus didn't say, "You *should* be salt" and "You *should* be light," or even that you *could* be salt and light. Rather, He said to His followers, "You *are* salt" and "You *are* light." While you might ask the Lord to make you saltier and help you shine brighter, you don't need to ask Him to make you salt and light. You already are. So get out of the shaker! Turn on your light!

Now, let's look more closely at each of Jesus's two illustrations.

Get Out of the Shaker

There are few things I like better at the end of a hard day than to sit and watch a movie while munching on popcorn. But a few weeks ago, I turned on the television and grabbed a handful of popcorn—only to realize as soon as I started chewing that I'd forgotten to add salt. Yuck! I couldn't wash it down with my Diet Coke fast enough.

No one likes bland popcorn—it's the salt that makes the difference. And though there was salt in my pantry, it wasn't doing any good as long as it stayed in my saltshaker.

Jesus compared believers to salt in the next part of His sermon:

> You are the salt of the earth; but if the salt has become tasteless, how can it be made salty again? It is no longer good for anything, except to be thrown out and trampled under foot by men. (Matt. 5:13)

46

So when Jesus said, "You are the salt of the earth," He meant we have to get out of the shaker—out of our holy huddles—and mingle with folks in the world. Just as salt that stays in the shaker isn't doing what it was created to do, believers who stay in their churches and Christian cliques aren't doing what they've been created to do.

And what have we been created to do? To shake and spread salt—to influence our world for good.

To appreciate Jesus's illustration here, we have to understand what salt was to Jesus's audience. In ancient days, salt was highly valued. The Greeks called it divine, and the Romans said, "There is nothing more useful than sun and salt."[3] Among other things, salt was (and still is) used to flavor food, create thirst in animals, cleanse objects, and fertilize land. It was even used as a form of currency.[4]

But in Jesus's time, there was an even more compelling reason for salt. In the days before refrigeration, salt was the only way to keep meat from spoiling. It was an invaluable commodity. So when Jesus called His disciples the salt of the earth, He was saying they were the preservative in this world. They were to make people thirsty for God and prevent the premature decay of the world.

That's as true for us today as it was in Jesus's time. I think you would agree that we are living in a culture that is decaying, wouldn't you? All we have to do is turn on the television or open an internet browser to know we are in a foul culture.

In my decades of experience as a pastor, I've noticed that Christians tend to go to one of two extremes when it comes to relating to the world. Some choose to isolate themselves from the culture. They huddle in their churches and Christian groups and say, "We have to protect ourselves from becoming defiled by the world." But Jesus doesn't want us to isolate ourselves from unbelievers. Instead, He said our goal should be to *influence* the culture. As "the salt of the earth," the only way we are going to spread our salt and make people thirsty for God is by getting out of the saltshaker and engaging with people who have differing points of view.

However, other Christians go to the opposite extreme. They say, "If I'm going to make a difference in this world, I need to identify with the culture. I'll show unbelievers that Christians are just like everybody else." But is that the way you influence the culture? If you become like everybody else, there is no distinctiveness to you.

In Jesus's day, most people couldn't afford to buy pure salt, so they would buy a mixture of salt and sand. And whenever people mixed salt with sand, there was a point at which the salt lost its effectiveness. That's why Jesus said, "If the salt has become tasteless, how can it be made salty again? It is no longer good for anything, except to be thrown out and trampled under foot by men" (v. 13). Notice what Jesus was saying here: whenever Christians start to adopt the attitudes and actions of the culture around us, we become watered-down and bland. We are no longer effective in preserving our families and communities, and others will no longer thirst for spiritual truths.

I can't tell you the number of Christians I've spoken with over the years who have become so contaminated with the world it is impossible to differentiate between their lifestyle and the lifestyle of the average non-Christian. And, as Jesus pointed out, salt contaminated with impurities loses its taste. The moment we lose our saltiness, our distinctiveness as Christians, we become useless for the cause of Christ in preserving our culture, in attracting unbelievers to the gospel, and in producing good works.

Jesus said that the way we live out our faith and influence our culture is not by becoming like the culture; it's by living in a way distinct from the culture. As "the salt of the earth," believers are to live out our faith in such a way that we preserve what is good and true in the world and slow the cultural rot we see all around us.

It's important to remember that even if you preserve meat with salt, eventually the meat decays and has to be discarded. In New Testament times, salt didn't *prevent* decay; it only *delayed* decay by giving meat a longer shelf life. Similarly, one of our functions as Christians here on earth is to stop the premature decay of society. When Jesus encouraged us to be "salt" in the world, He was reminding us that while we will never be able to reverse the decay caused by the curse of sin, we can slow down the process by how we live and what we do.[5]

I have two questions for you before moving on. First, *How do you taste?* Are you salty? Do you have non-Christian friends who sense something distinctive in you? Is the way you are living causing others to thirst after the Christ you are serving?

Second, *Are you stuck in the saltshaker?* Do you spend all your time with other Christians, without taking opportunities to talk with unbelievers? If so, then it's time to get out and let the world taste the goodness of Christ, just as David wrote: "O taste and see that the LORD is good" (Ps. 34:8).

Turn On Your Light

Bible teacher William Barclay said the greatest compliment you can give someone is to call them "the salt of the earth," but the greatest compliment you can give a Christian is to say they are "the light of the world"—because that's how Jesus described Himself in John 9:5.[6] It's a way of saying, "You're just like Jesus," which is God's purpose for every believer. That's why Jesus said to His followers,

> You are the light of the world. A city set on a hill cannot be hidden; nor does anyone light a lamp and put it under a basket, but on the lampstand, and it gives light to all who are in the house. (Matt. 5:14–15)

No doubt about it: we are living in a world full of darkness—full of immorality, deception, unbelief, corruption, violence, and pain. But when we live out our faith by being the Beatitudes, the light of Christ pierces the darkness and dispels it. The reason God has left us here on earth is so that we can spread the light of the gospel in this dark world.

To illustrate His teaching, Jesus used two images of light His listeners would easily understand. First, He likened believers to a shining hilltop city. He said, "A city set on a hill cannot be hidden" (v. 14). At the time, Israel was a rural nation. Small villages dotted the landscape, but there was only one major city, and it sat atop a prominent hill. At night, when lights shone from Jerusalem's houses and the temple, the city could be seen for miles around.

The image of a shining city in the darkness reminds me of my first position as senior pastor, which was in a church in the small West Texas town of Eastland. We loved our time there, but the town was isolated from any metropolis, making the nights unusually dark. When I had to travel at night to Dallas to visit my parents, I would begin to see the lights of the Dallas–Fort Worth metroplex miles before I reached the city limits. I think that is what Jesus meant when He compared Christians to a shining city on a hill.

Think of it like this: you've probably seen satellite images from outer space showing sections of the United States at night. You can always pick out such metropolitan centers as Boston, New York, Philadelphia, and Washington, DC, on the East Coast, or Seattle, San Francisco, Los Angeles, and San Diego on the West Coast. There are a few bright lights in the middle of the country—Chicago, Dallas–Fort Worth, Austin, San Antonio, and Houston—but there are lots of dark areas. Whether traveling at night or looking at a dark satellite image, we are attracted to the light. And that's just what our lives are meant to be: lights that attract those living in darkness.

Jesus not only likened believers to bright hilltop cities but also said we are like lit lamps (v. 15). In Jesus's day, lamps were made from clay and looked sort of like the genie's lamp in *Aladdin*. There was a cavity that held a reservoir of oil in which one end of a wick soaked, and the other end of the wick stuck out the neck of the lamp. Lamps were usually placed on a wooden lampstand to light a room, as Jesus said. No one covered a lamp; that would defeat the purpose of lighting it. In the same way, Jesus said, hiding our light defeats the purpose of following Him. As a friend of mine likes to say, "None of us works for the CIA—Christian Incognito Association." The reason Jesus enlightens us, by indwelling us with the Holy Spirit, is so we will shine.

The apostle Paul picked up on this analogy of light in Philippians 2:15–16 when he said that Christians "appear as lights in the world, holding fast the word of life." Instead of having a negative, fatalistic attitude about the dark culture in which we live, Paul urged us to see this life as an opportunity to shine the light of Christ and spread the gospel. After all, the darker the background, the brighter the light.

Now, it's important to remember that no matter how bright your light for Christ may be, it cannot dispel the darkness unless it comes into contact with the darkness. Imagine that your electricity goes out late one night, and you need to check your breaker. It's pitch black in your house, so you grab a flashlight on your way to the breaker box. However, if you say, "I don't want to offend the darkness" and put that flashlight in your pocket, then its light isn't going to do you any good. The only way the darkness will be dispelled is if your light collides with it.

It's the same way with each of us. The reason God has placed you in your job, in your school, in your neighborhood, or within a certain group of friends is so that you can shine your spiritual light and influence them for God. We live in a world where millions of people are lost in spiritual darkness. Though many of them love the darkness (John 3:19), our mission is to shine the light of the gospel.

How do we do that? Jesus told us in Matthew 5:16,

Let your light shine before men in such a way that they may see your good works, and glorify your Father who is in heaven.

Our faith, as we practice it in the world, is to consist of not only right beliefs but also right behaviors. Jesus called these "good works," which include everything we say and do because we bear the name of Christ.

In the New Testament Greek, there are two words translated as "good." The first, *agathos*, describes the quality of something, while the second, *kalos*, describes both the quality and the attractiveness of something. So if I said, "That's a good [*agathos*] apple," it would mean the apple is fresh. But if I said, "That's a good [*kalos*] apple," I would be saying the apple is fresh *and* looks good enough to eat.

When Jesus said, "That they may see your good works," He used *kalos*, meaning that our good works should not only bear the stamp of *quality* but should also be *appealing*. Consider this: How does your Christian walk appear to outsiders? Do they see you begrudgingly obeying God with a rotten attitude, or are your good works appealing to others, causing them to want to know more about your faith? Remember, our attractiveness is not to draw attention to ourselves but to draw attention to God, so others might "glorify [our] Father who is in heaven" (v. 16).

These two metaphors—salt and light—create an intriguing image of what Christians should be and do. They balance each other. Salt is *invisible*, working slowly and secretly. It's negative in that it delays spiritual decay within our society. Light, on the other hand, is *visible*, working quickly and openly. It's positive in that it offers a lighted path toward forgiveness and salvation for our society.

How can you apply this in your life? Easy. Is your workplace dark and bland? Is your school or neighborhood filled with darkness and spiritual decay? Then shine the light of Christ and add a little spiritual flavor to it. You don't want to blind others or dump a truckload of salt on them by quoting the Bible at them constantly. Remember, too much salt ruins the food, and too much light blinds the eyes. So, as pastor and author Chuck Swindoll put it, "Shake, don't pour. Shine, don't blind."[7]

Submit and Surpass

Jesus expanded on the idea of good works in verses 17–20. But in these verses, instead of calling it "good works," He called it "righteousness."

Now, *righteousness* is another one of those Christianese words we throw around without really knowing what it means. The word *righteous* is used a few different ways in the Bible. Sometimes it refers to *imputed righteousness*—the right standing we receive from God as a gift when we trust in Jesus Christ as our Savior. But as we saw in chapter 1, there is a second kind of righteousness in the Bible, and that is *ethical righteousness*. Ethical righteousness refers to how we conduct our lives after we are saved.

Put another way: while imputed righteousness is our *right standing* before God, ethical righteousness is our *right acting* before God. In this sense, *righteousness* is a word for right living. And that is the righteousness Jesus was talking about in the Sermon on the Mount.

This idea of righteousness is a primary theme throughout this sermon. In the Beatitudes, Jesus explained what a righteous disciple *is*. In His illustrations of salt and light, Jesus explained what a righteous disciple *does*. Starting with verse 17, Jesus clarified the idea of right living. This clarification was important because the religious leaders of the day misinterpreted and misapplied what they viewed as the "righteousness" of good works. And so do we.

But in this section of Scripture, Jesus did more than just define Christian righteousness and how it should be practiced. He also threw light on the relationship between the Old and New Testaments, between the law and the gospel.

In Matthew 5:17–18, Jesus explained His relationship to the law, and then in verses 19–20, He talked about His followers' relationship to the law.

Submit to the Scripture

If righteousness is the process of conforming our character and conduct to the will of God, then the foundation of our righteousness is the Word of God. And that's what Jesus addressed next:

> Do not think that I came to abolish the Law or the Prophets; I did not come to abolish but to fulfill. (Matt. 5:17)

Jesus's opening statement, "Do not think that I came to abolish the Law or the Prophets," may come out of the blue to our ears, but it wouldn't have surprised His original audience. In his Gospel, Mark indicated that a controversy surrounding the Sabbath occurred early in Jesus's ministry, before the Sermon on the Mount (2:23–26). So there were likely some Pharisees in the audience who questioned Jesus's understanding of God's Word, believing He was radical and unorthodox. Since much of what Jesus wanted to talk about in this sermon involved His interpretation of and relationship to the law, Jesus needed to address this controversy head-on.

Before we can fully appreciate what Jesus meant about not abolishing the law but fulfilling it, let me make a few observations. First of all, Jews in the first century divided the Old Testament into three general sections: the Law (the five books of Moses), the Prophets (the writings of the major and minor prophets), and the Psalms (including the Wisdom

Literature of Job, Proverbs, Song of Solomon, and Eccle-siastes). But when they used the phrase "the Law and the Prophets," they were referring to the entire Old Testament.[8]

Second, notice that Jesus used the verb "come" twice in Matthew 5:17: "I *came* . . . I did not *come*." His word choice here was no accident. *Come* had messianic overtones, refer-ring to the one who was to fulfill the Old Testament promises of the Messiah.

Jesus went on to say about His relationship to the Law and the Prophets, "I did not come to abolish but to fulfill" (v. 17). The phrase "to fulfill" here has the same meaning as used in Matthew 2:15, where Jesus, as a child, returned to Israel from Egypt "to fulfill what had been spoken" by the prophet Hosea. The idea is that Jesus would accomplish everything that was written about the Messiah in the Old Testament.

Finally, for the first time in His sermon, Jesus referred to Himself personally. In the Beatitudes, He spoke in the third person. When He talked about salt and light, He spoke in the second person. But now, Jesus spoke in the first person be-cause the Pharisees were questioning whether Jesus's words had more authority than the Scriptures. He said, "Do not think that I came to abolish the Law or the Prophets; I did not come to abolish but to fulfill" (v. 17).

Jesus was saying that He had come to fulfill the Word of God completely. I think of it like this: on May 30, 2020, I watched with anticipation the launch of NASA's SpaceX *Crew Dragon*, the first manned space flight to launch from American soil since July 2011. But before the rocket was launched from the pad, there was a lengthy checklist to go through. If any item on the list could not be checked off as completed, the flight would have been scrubbed.

In a similar manner, the Old Testament contains doctrines, ethical standards, and prophecies about the coming Messiah. Jesus checked all the boxes completely and flawlessly. He perfectly obeyed the law's demands, He interpreted its words as God originally intended, and He fulfilled all the prophecies relating to the Messiah. He did all these things with the highest admiration for the inspired and inerrant Word of God.

However, the scribes and Pharisees of Jesus's day were distorting God's Word. They determined that the law of Moses contained 248 commandments and 365 prohibitions. But in the process of interpreting and defining these commands, the religious leaders came up with thousands of additional rules and regulations. For example, in Exodus 20:9–10, the Lord said, "Six days you shall labor and do all your work, but the seventh day is a sabbath of the LORD your God; in it you shall not do any work." But what exactly did it mean to "work"? To answer that question, the scribes and Pharisees developed rules to regulate the Sabbath. For example, they said you couldn't write because the action of writing was considered work. But what constituted writing? The religious leaders defined it as, "He who writes two letters of the alphabet with his right or with his left hand, whether of one kind or of two kinds, if they are written with different inks or in different languages, is guilty."[9]

And on and on it went, with every little detail about life. This is what Jesus had no patience for. He wouldn't change or cancel God's law, but He wouldn't put up with the nonsense of the scribes and Pharisees, who, by adding layers of rules and regulations, made a mockery of God's law.

Unlike the religious leaders who believed their interpretations were equal to God's Word, Jesus said nothing was equal to God's Word—not even heaven and earth—and He would uphold even the smallest features of the Old Testament. He continued,

> For truly I say to you, until heaven and earth pass away, not the smallest letter or stroke shall pass from the Law until all is accomplished. (Matt. 5:18)

To understand what Jesus was saying here, we need to know something about the Greek alphabet of the New Testament and the Hebrew alphabet of the Old Testament. The King James Version translates Jesus's phrase "smallest letter or stroke" in verse 18 as "one jot or one tittle"—literally, "one iota or one horn." The *iota* (ι) was the smallest letter in the Greek alphabet. It also represents the smallest letter in the Hebrew alphabet, the *yod* (י). If you think that's small, the tittle (or horn) is even smaller. In Hebrew, some letters are identical except for a tiny stroke, or tittle, attached to the stem of the letter. For example, the only difference between the letters *waw* (ו), *daleth* (ד), and *resh* (ר) is the little flare at the end of each letter. In fact, when I took Hebrew in seminary many years ago, students actually brought magnifying glasses to class so they could identify certain letters by the presence or absence of such strokes!

Jesus was saying that things we believe to be timeless and permanent, like the universe, are transitory compared to the smallest letter of a word and the minutest strokes found on the letters that comprise those words in Scripture. It's as if Jesus were saying, "The authority of Scripture is so great that the whole universe will be wiped from existence before one dot above an *i* or one cross of a *t* passes away and until every part of God's Word has been fulfilled, which is what I am here to do."

Why is it important today that the authority of Scripture is greater than the universe itself? In a culture that seems to be constantly changing its mind about what is acceptable and right, Jesus's teaching reminds us that we must bring our opinions about the validity of other religions, same-sex relationships, abortion, capital punishment, or any other controversial subject under the authority of God's Word. Then, we are to articulate and represent God's views to those within God's kingdom and those living outside of it.

Surpassing the Pharisees

Using a play on words, Jesus continued His teaching about how the scribes and Pharisees misapplied the Scripture in verse 19. He said,

> Whoever then annuls one of the *least* of these command-ments, and teaches others to do the same, shall be called *least* in the kingdom of heaven; but whoever keeps and teaches them, he shall be called great in the kingdom of heaven.

As if they were beef inspectors, Jewish rabbis graded the Old Testament commands according to which ones they believed were most authoritative and, therefore, most im-portant to obey and teach. The command to love God and love your neighbor might be stamped as Prime (the highest grade), while the command to wash your hands for various reasons might be stamped as Select (a much lower grade). Jesus rejected this view. To Him, all of Scripture was equally authoritative and equally important to obey and teach.

What does it mean to be called "great" in the kingdom of heaven? Greatness in God's eyes is our ability to conform our character and conduct to the Word of God. This is what Jesus meant by "righteousness" in verse 20:

> For I say to you that unless your righteousness surpasses that of the scribes and Pharisees, you will not enter the kingdom of heaven.

In Jesus's time, no one was regarded as more pious than the scribes and Pharisees. But Jesus knew the religious leaders were hypocrites, obeying some commands and disregarding others. Such selective obedience produced superficial righteousness, focused on external conformity instead of internal character. That wouldn't do, Jesus said, for anyone wanting to enter the kingdom of heaven. Selective obedience reveals a heart that is in rebellion against God.

For example, if you have teenagers at home, as Amy and I once did, you understand this concept. Suppose you have a list of "house rules" for your kids that includes doing their homework on time, cleaning their rooms, and not drinking alcoholic beverages. One evening, you receive a phone call from the police informing you that your teen has been arrested for drunk driving. When you begin to lambaste your child for his or her behavior, imagine your teenager responds by saying, "What's the big deal? I did my homework this week, and my room is spotless!" I doubt you would be any more impressed by that defense than God is by our rationalization for sin based on selective obedience.

Obviously, none of us are able to obey all of God's laws completely. As James wrote, "For whoever keeps the whole law and yet stumbles in one point, he has become guilty of all" (2:10). We all engage in "selective obedience" when it comes to God's standards, and because of that, we are all guilty before God. That is why everyone from the pastor to the prostitute is desperately in need of God's forgiveness.

But don't use God's grace as an excuse for disobedience. After we have received God's pardon for our sin and received His power to be free from sin, we are not permitted to treat God's standards like a spiritual buffet—selecting what we like and leaving the rest for someone else. Conduct flows out of character. So, as Jesus explained, we are to demonstrate our faith by our right living, with attitudes and actions that reflect the character of Christ.

Dos and Don'ts

In Matthew 5:13–20, Jesus called us to a radical faith—to be salt and light in a decaying and darkening world, to submit to the authority of Scripture, and to surpass the righteousness of the scribes and Pharisees. To help you do that, let me give you two don'ts and two dos.

First, *don't draw attention to yourself.* Remember, your purpose as a Christian is to put the spotlight on Christ, not on yourself. When you live your life in wholehearted obedience to the Word of God, others will see your good works and glorify God.

Second, *don't hold back or hide under.* If there is one thing that unbelievers living dark and decaying lives need to taste and see, it is people of faith. So get out of the shaker and turn on your light!

Third, *do take the Word of God seriously*. In 2 Timothy 3:16–17, the apostle Paul wrote, "All Scripture is inspired by God and profitable for teaching, for reproof, for correction, for training in righteousness; so that the man of God may be adequate, equipped for every good work." God doesn't play around when it comes to His Word, and neither should we.

Finally, *do follow the Word of God faithfully*. For Christians, the Bible is the absolute rule of faith and life. There may be other sources of wisdom we can learn from, but Scripture is the only source of true righteousness. Believing God's Word and obeying God's Word are inseparably linked. As someone once said, "To believe but not to obey is not to believe at all." But when you consistently follow God's commands, you will become the salt that creates spiritual thirst in others and the light that illuminates the path to Jesus Christ.

three

Straight Talk about Your Relationships

HOWARD HENDRICKS, my mentor and seminary professor, used to tell students on the verge of graduating from seminary and setting out into the world of vocational ministry, "Remember, the higher the monkey goes, the more his rear end shows." His warning was obvious but often forgotten by those in positions of leadership: increased power and influence bring increased scrutiny and criticism.

I can vouch for the wisdom of Dr. Hendricks's counsel. As somebody whose preaching is broadcast on radio and television, who writes books, and who is often asked to comment on current events from a Christian perspective on nationally televised news outlets, I get my fair share of critics. I've been accused of being everything from a hypocrite to a false teacher to a huckster whose only motivation is to turn a buck. And these are some of the kindest things I've been called! Other terms are . . . well, "not fit subjects for Christians to talk about" (Eph. 5:3 Phillips).

Dr. Hendricks also encouraged his students to develop a tough hide while maintaining a soft heart. That's easily said but not easily done—trust me. But after many years in ministry in somewhat of a spotlight, I've come to appreciate this comment by Abraham Lincoln: "When a man hears himself somewhat misrepresented, it provokes him . . . but when the misrepresentation becomes very gross and palpable, it is more apt to amuse him."[1]

I bring this up not because I'm looking for sympathy— believe me, I'm not. Over the years, I've developed a hide as tough as a rhinoceros's. But there are many who have learned the hard way that the saying "Sticks and stones may break my bones, but words will never hurt me" is a lie. In fact, some of the worst bruises and breaks come from words hurled in anger. Many people you know are carrying inside them a crushed spirit. They are your neighbors and friends, your family members, maybe even your spouse or yourself. They are adults who carry childhood wounds from parents whose words bruised and slapped. They are children or teenagers who think about ways to end their lives—and too many who carry out those plans—because of bullies at school or online.

There is a reason Solomon wrote, "Like apples of gold in settings of silver is a word spoken in right circumstances" (Prov. 25:11) and Paul said, "Let your speech always be with grace, as though seasoned with salt, so that you will know how you should respond to each person" (Col. 4:6). Words are more potent than poison. And this is the next point Jesus made in His Sermon on the Mount.

An Overview of Radical Righteousness

In chapter 2, we looked at Jesus's command for our righteousness, or right living, to "[surpass] that of the scribes and Pharisees" (Matt. 5:20). I have no doubt this statement was shocking to His original audience, since they considered the scribes and Pharisees to be the embodiment of righteousness. But Jesus knew better, and He exposed these religious leaders as being concerned only with external actions and disregarding internal attitudes.

As we have seen, the righteousness Jesus was talking about in the Sermon on the Mount is allowing God's Word to change both our *attitudes* and *actions*. How can we do that? To make His teaching practical, Jesus gave six examples in Matthew 5:

- murder (vv. 21–26)
- adultery (vv. 27–30)
- divorce (vv. 31–32)
- oaths (vv. 33–37)
- retaliation (vv. 38–42)
- love (vv. 43–47)

We won't look at all six topics in this chapter, but an overview of the common elements among them will help us understand just how radical Jesus's call to righteousness was (and is).

In each of Jesus's examples, the scribes and Pharisees failed to understand the Old Testament and therefore failed the test of true righteousness. Jesus introduced each topic with "You have heard," or "It was said," and then He quoted the Old Testament or the traditional teaching of the day, which the religious leaders considered to be just as authoritative as Scripture.

"You have heard" was a common expression among first-century rabbis to refer to the Old Testament. The Old Testament prophets before them often introduced their pronouncements with "Thus says the Lord." But no prophet or rabbi ever claimed authority on his own—that is, until Jesus came along with "*But I say.*" With this controversial phrase, Jesus not only called into question the authority of the religious leaders but also put His words on an equal footing with Scripture. Throughout His ministry, Jesus claimed to be God in at least twelve different ways, one of which was to teach truth on His own authority, as He did throughout the Sermon on the Mount.[2]

Jesus's teaching was revolutionary—so much so that after His sermon, the crowd sat in stunned silence. Matthew recorded, "When Jesus had finished these words, the crowds were amazed at His teaching; for He was teaching them as one having authority, and not as their scribes" (7:28–29). Jesus's call to righteousness in this talk was like nothing the people had ever heard, and it began with His call to demonstrate radical righteousness in our relationships.

Murder by Hand

Jesus's first example of how the scribes and Pharisees failed to understand the Scripture, and therefore failed to live up to God's standard of righteousness, was based on the sixth commandment. In this example, Jesus linked a command from the Lord with the civil law of Moses:

You have heard that the ancients were told, "You shall not commit murder" and "Whoever commits murder shall be liable to the court." (Matt. 5:21)

The court Jesus referred to was a local judicial body where those found guilty of murder were sentenced to death (Num. 35:30–31).

The Pharisees correctly interpreted that those who committed murder deserved capital punishment. Scripture is clear that God, who is the Giver of life, values human life so much that if anyone is guilty of taking a life out of anger or convenience, that person shall be punished by death—a command that predates the Mosaic law. In Genesis 9:6, God said to Noah, "Whoever sheds man's blood, by man his blood shall be shed, for in the image of God He made man." But the Pharisees' understanding of God's Word extended only to the *act* of murder, not to the *attitudes* that led to murder. They believed that as long as they never physically committed homicide, they were righteous.

"Not so fast," Jesus said, in effect. According to Jesus, the command "do not murder" has a much wider application than merely refraining from the act of murder. It includes thoughts and words, anger and insults, as well as spilling blood. It's sort of like when my daughters were younger, and I had to instruct one to tell the other she was sorry for pushing her sister to the ground. When she responded with a perfunctory "Sorry," I said to her, "It's not enough just to *say* you're sorry. You've got to actually *be* sorry." The difference transforms the act of mouthing the right words to conveying the right attitude of repentance. In the same way, it's not enough just not to commit murder; you have to not even *want* to commit murder.

"Well, that's easy enough," you may be saying. "I'd never actually kill anybody. So what does this teaching have to do with me?" Everything.

Jesus's teaching in this passage is one of the Bible's foundational passages on human relationships. Yes, murder is an extreme severing of a relationship, but there are other kinds of fractures that can be just as destructive. That's what Jesus went on to address in His talk—the attitudes that reveal what righteousness *really* looks like when it comes to our relationships.

Murder in the Heart

Jesus explained that the sixth commandment—"You shall not murder" (Exod. 20:13)—was intended not only as a prohibition against homicide but also as a prohibition against hate. Murderers commit murder a thousand times in their hearts before they commit one murder with their hands.

Jesus said,

> But I say to you that everyone who is angry with his brother shall be guilty before the court; and whoever says to his brother, "You good-for-nothing," shall be guilty before the supreme court; and whoever says, "You fool," shall be guilty enough to go into the fiery hell. (Matt. 5:22)

In this example, He identified three specific ways we might be guilty of murder in our hearts: anger, insults, and defamation.

Anger: "I'll Kill You!"

Henry Fonda was one of the best actors of his age. In 1957, Fonda played one of twelve men on a jury who had to determine the guilt or innocence of a young man on trial for the murder of his father.

As the jurors discussed the case, the character of each man was revealed, most notably the anger of a man who wanted to take out his hatred on the defendant for something his own teenage son had done. Much of the jurors' discussion surrounded what the young man supposedly yelled just before stabbing his father to death: "I'll kill you!"

Fonda's character didn't put much stock in the expression. He argued that we say things like that all the time and don't literally mean it. "I could kill you for that, darling," Fonda said. "Junior, you do that once more and I'll kill you."

In the climax of the movie, Fonda and the angry juror, played by Lee J. Cobb, confront each other. Fonda said, "Are you his executioner?"

"I'm one of 'em," Cobb said.

"Perhaps you'd like to pull the switch."

"For this kid, you bet I would."

"I feel sorry for you," Fonda said. "What it must feel like to wanna pull the switch! Ever since you walked into this room, you've been acting like a self-appointed public avenger. You want to see this boy die because you personally want it, not because of the facts. You're a sadist."

At that, Cobb lunged for Fonda, crying out, "I'll kill him! I'll kill him!"

"You don't really mean you'll kill me, do you?" Fonda said.[3]

All of this is played out to powerful effect in *Twelve Angry Men*. It is true, as Fonda's character points out, that we can say, "I'll kill you" and mean nothing more by it than to express our displeasure. But there are times when it expresses uncontrollable anger, the kind of rage Jesus said makes us "guilty before the court" (v. 22).

It's helpful to understand that there are two Greek words for anger. The first word, *thymos*, expresses a flash of anger. Like a grass fire, *thymos* is the kind of anger that burns intensely but quickly, then it's gone. The other word is *orge*, which refers to a slow-building and long-lasting type of anger. This is the kind of anger that one nurses, broods over, and keeps warm through thoughts of revenge. *Orge* is like a fire that starts in the attic and builds, consuming more and more until the entire house is ablaze. This is the anger Jesus was speaking about in Matthew 5:22.

Orge is the anger I addressed in my book *Invincible*, when I described Cain's downward spiral into murder. He was first envious of his brother Abel, because Abel's sacrifice to the Lord was acceptable and Cain's wasn't (Gen. 4:4–5). Then Cain's envy turned into unrighteous anger that he stewed over until it turned into bitterness. And once Cain had that taste in his mouth, he murdered Abel (v. 8).[4]

Those who express this type of anger aren't necessarily likely to kill somebody, but they can consider others dead to them. I've counseled those who have been disowned by family members because they violated some principle held sacred within the family. For example, I know a Christian man in his midfifties who recently told his mother that he drinks beer or has a glass of wine on occasion. She views drinking as a mortal sin and in her anger refuses to have anything to do with her son. Whatever your position is on Christians drinking alcohol, this mother's reaction is extreme, and in her self-righteous anger she has killed her son in her heart.

Insults: "You're an Idiot!"

Unrighteous anger is just one illustration of what we might call "spiritual murder." Another is to hurl insults at people.

Jesus went on to say, "Whoever says to his brother, 'You good-for-nothing,' shall be guilty before the supreme court" (Matt. 5:22). That phrase "good-for-nothing" is the Aramaic word *raca*. Literally, it means "empty." When applied to a person, it refers to someone's mental abilities—saying a person is empty-headed. Today, we might use words like *nitwit*, *airhead*, or what Lucy often called Charlie Brown, *blockhead*. The word *raca* includes not just the insult itself but also the tone of voice behind the insult—expressing contempt for another person. I mean, just say the word *raca* out loud. It sounds angry and contemptuous, and that's what Jesus was warning against.

You see, there's more than one way to kill a person. We can destroy human life not only through physical violence but also through our words. That's why Jesus made the connection between physical murder and the harmful words we speak to another person. When you verbally assault someone, you're verbally assaulting God's creation.

James said, "No one can tame the tongue; it is a restless evil and full of deadly poison. With it we bless our Lord and Father, and with it we curse men, who have been made in the likeness of God; from the same mouth come both blessing and cursing. My brethren, these things ought not to be this way" (3:8–10).

When we curse somebody, we are cursing someone made in the image of God.

By the way, just because someone is not a Christian does not give us the right to assault that person verbally. I recall a politician who made news when he called a senator from New York a "schmuck." There was a lot of discussion about the Yiddish meaning of *schmuck*. Is it an obscene term, or does it just mean "jerk"? Regardless, it's a derisive term. And no matter how unrighteous that senator may be, he is still a human being God created.

I've been guilty of the very same thing. In some act of righteous indignation I thought I was so right and the other person was so wrong, especially if the person was a non-Christian, that I felt as if I had the right to demean the person with my words. No, Jesus said. Whenever we attack another person verbally, we are attacking someone whom God made.

Every person is made in God's image. After all, think about how God looks at us. Jesus Christ had every reason to question our worth, didn't He? In light of our sin, He could have demeaned us. But He didn't do that. Instead, because of the great love He had for us, Jesus looked beyond our faults. He died for us and offered us forgiveness. We are to treat others the same way. Don't be guilty of murder by words, which doesn't reflect the righteousness of God.

Defamation: "You Fool!"

Jesus rounded out this portion of His teaching regarding righteousness in relationships with this final warning: "Whoever says, 'You fool,' shall be guilty enough to go into the fiery hell" (Matt. 5:22).

The Greek word Jesus used here for "fool" is *moros*, from which we get our word *moron*. Whereas *raca* is aimed at a person's intellect, *moros* is aimed at a person's character. It tarnishes a person's name and reputation and brands that person a moral reprobate.

One of the most striking examples of this comes from our nation's history. In the 1800 election between president John Adams and vice president Thomas Jefferson, Jefferson hired newspaperman James Callender to run a series of articles attacking Adams. Critics of Adams accused him of being a monarchist and warmonger, but Callender added to the list, calling Adams a "repulsive pedant," a "gross hypocrite" who was "in his private life, one of the most egregious fools upon the continent," and a "strange compound of ignorance and ferocity, of deceit, and weakness."[5]

Today, we call that character assassination. Solomon wrote, "A good name is to be more desired than great wealth" (Prov. 22:1), and "With his mouth the godless man destroys his neighbor" (11:9). Jesus said anyone who destroys another person's name and reputation through defamation is liable for eternal damnation.

Now, Jesus wasn't saying that those who practice such unrighteousness in their relationships *will* go to hell. Rather, He said those who hold unjustified anger against another or insult others or defame them are guilty *enough* to be *sent* to hell. He simply used multiple examples to make a point: every death wish that robs people of their humanity is sufficient to receive the strictest judgment from God.

But What about Jesus?

You may be wondering, *What about Jesus? Didn't He get angry? And doesn't the Bible say the Lord hates certain things?* He did, and it does. In fact, later in Matthew's Gospel, Jesus called the Pharisees "fools" (23:17). So what are we to think about this apparent contradiction when it comes to anger and hate?

If you look carefully at the passages that speak of God hating something—such as Psalms 5:5–6; 11:5; and Proverbs 6:16–19—you'll discover that God hates the wicked *attitudes* and *actions* of people, not the people themselves. When Jesus got angry, whether at the grave of Lazarus (John 11:33, 38) or while cleansing the temple (2:13–16), He demonstrated a righteous anger to preserve the things of God: life and the integrity of worship.

And when Jesus called the Pharisees "fools," He was addressing the fact that they were mishandling and maligning the Scripture they claimed to defend. They were lying about what God's Word actually said regarding taking oaths, and in that they were acting immorally.

Jesus's anger was always righteous because it was, as Martin Luther observed, "an anger of love, one that wishes no one any evil, one that is friendly to the person but hostile to the sin."[6]

Two Illustrations of Radical Reconciliation

Jesus brought home His straight talk about righteousness in our relationships by offering two illustrations that are just as practical for us today as they were for His original audience more than two thousand years ago.

"Be Reconciled to Your Brother"

In His first illustration, Jesus described temple worship and stressed the importance of reconciliation over worship. He said,

Therefore if you are presenting your offering at the altar, and there remember that your brother has something against you, leave your offering there before the altar and go; first be reconciled to your brother, and then come and present your offering. (Matt. 5:23–24)

In the temple in Jerusalem, the Jewish people passed through a series of courtyards with their sacrifices—the Court of Gentiles, the Court of Women, and the Court of Men—before finally reaching the Court of the Priests. The worshipers weren't permitted to enter there, so they handed their sacrifices to the priest, who would place it on the brass altar. However, as Jesus said, if worshipers suddenly realized they had somehow offended a brother or sister, they should leave the sacrifice with the priest and "first be reconciled" to their brother or sister before coming back to the temple to make their offering.

"Wait a minute, Pastor," you may be saying. "Since you're already at the temple, why not just finish making your offering there and then go make things right with the other person?" Jesus had a radical perspective on repairing broken relationships. He said relieving a brother or sister of the anger and hatred that might be welling up in his or her heart because of some offense is more important, at that moment, than worshiping God. In other words, internal purity is more important than external piety.

This is one of the few times in the Bible we are commanded to interrupt our worship for something more important: reconciliation. As the apostle Paul said in 2 Corinthians 5:18–19, "God . . . reconciled us to Himself through Christ and gave us the ministry of reconciliation, namely, that God was in Christ reconciling the world to Himself, not counting their trespasses against them, and He has committed to us the word of reconciliation."

I heard that one pastor, while preaching on Matthew 5:21–26, paused after reading verses 23–24 and said to the church, which had a lot of infighting, "Now, go and do it. Right now, this very minute"—and he meant it. The sermon and the rest of the worship service recommenced only after the congregation made things right with one another. That was a daring thing to do, but that's exactly what Jesus meant.

Let me ask you: Does someone have something against you because you've hurt them in some way, and you need to make amends? If so, before you attend another Sunday worship service, make sure you've reached out for reconciliation first, then you can worship God with a clean conscience. You'll demonstrate a righteousness that surpasses that of the scribes and Pharisees if you do.

"Make Friends Quickly with Your Opponent"

Jesus's second illustration involved a civil court proceeding and stressed the importance of making things right quickly. He said,

> Make friends quickly with your opponent at law while you are with him on the way, so that your opponent may not hand you over to the judge, and the judge to the officer, and you be thrown into prison. Truly I say to you, you will not come out of there until you have paid up the last cent. (Matt. 5:25–26)

In the ancient world, and even until the 1830s in America, those who failed to pay their debts could be brought before the court by lenders and forced to go to debtor's prison. This is the situation Jesus described in verses 25–26. Before you ever darken the courthouse doors, Jesus said, you should make every effort to settle your debts and make amends with the one who is now your opponent. While you are outside the courtroom, there may be an opportunity to plead for more time or for the forgiveness of the debt. But as soon as you stand before the judge unable to pay, the judge has no choice but to hand you over to the bailiff, who hands you over to the jailer.

Jesus's point is applicable to any offense we've caused somebody. Whatever the offense may be, we should quickly "make friends" with our opponent, because if we don't, then troubles begin to pile up, making things worse. For example, Amy and I rarely argue. But when we do, it's usually my fault. However, I have found that if I go to her soon after our argument and ask for forgiveness, she's more likely to forgive me on the spot. If I wait, stewing in my self-righteousness while she stews in her hurt and anger, then it becomes harder for me to ask for forgiveness and harder for her to extend it.

So remember these two principles:

1. Reconciliation is more powerful than revenge.
2. Reconciling today is wiser than reconciling tomorrow.

John Taylor, a contemporary of William Shakespeare, wrote, "Pens are most dangerous tools, more sharp by odds than swords, and cut more keen than whips or rods."[7] Sticks and stones may indeed break bones, but words can wound and kill. So if you want to honor God in your relationships, watch your tongue, and when it gets away from you, work for reconciliation—and do so *quickly*.

77

four

Straight Talk about Your Sex Life

I'M NOT A GARDENER, but I know enough about gardening to know that dedicated gardeners don't treat weeds with kindness; they declare war on them. They'll eradicate any invasive plant that might creep into their garden and choke out the life of their pansies or petunias, cucumbers or kumquats. The late Swedish diplomat and former secretary-general of the United Nations Dag Hammarskjöld was correct in saying, "He who wants to keep his garden tidy doesn't reserve a plot for weeds."[1]

However, Hammarskjöld wasn't giving advice on gardening; he was giving advice on tending to our moral lives. He wrote, "You cannot play with the animal in you without becoming wholly animal, play with falsehood without forfeiting your right to truth, play with cruelty without losing your sensitivity of mind."[2] He could have added, "You cannot play with sexual immorality without losing your fidelity to your spouse."

It's all too easy to neglect our marriages and allow invasive "weeds" to grow. And the largest threat to any marriage is sexual immorality—the topic Jesus discussed next in His message on radical righteousness.

Remember, the righteousness Jesus was talking about in the Sermon on the Mount has to do with conforming our character and conduct to God's Word, not to the standards of the scribes and Pharisees. In this passage, Jesus taught His followers the right living that honors God in our relationships.

A Radical Call to Sexual Fidelity

In the previous chapter, we looked at the first illustration Jesus gave of radical righteousness, taken from the sixth commandment, which prohibits murder. Next, He gave a second illustration about righteousness in our relationships, taken from the seventh commandment, which prohibits adultery (Exod. 20:14).

Adultery in the Bed

Using the same formula He did when introducing the illustration of murder, Jesus said,

> You have heard that it was said, "You shall not commit adultery." (Matt. 5:27)

The rabbis in Jesus's day were correct in their general interpretation of adultery: having sex with another person outside the bounds of marriage is a violation of God's Word and worthy of punishment. Jesus was okay with that. But just like the rabbis' interpretation of murder, their interpretation of adultery focused only on the external act, not on the internal attitude that led to the act. And Jesus wasn't okay with *that*.

The scribes and Pharisees recognized that the tenth commandment—which includes the phrase "you shall not covet your neighbor's wife" (Exod. 20:17)—alluded to the internal aspect of adultery by prohibiting covetousness of another person's mate. But they tended to focus only on the external act. This led to a narrow definition of sexual sin. In their system, you either committed the physical act of adultery or you didn't. And if you were caught in the act of adultery, then you were stoned to death (Lev. 20:10).

The scribes and Pharisees believed that as long as they avoided having extramarital sex, they were fulfilling God's commands. Their brand of righteousness focused solely on external actions, so when they succeeded by not physically committing adultery, they basked in the glow of their own self-righteousness and assumed they had the approval of God—until Jesus came along.

Adultery in the Head

Years ago, when I was a youth minister, I shared with our youth group what I call "The Four Rules of Dating" to follow if they wanted to avoid sexual immorality:

1. Don't pull up.
2. Don't pull down.

3. Don't unbutton.

4. Don't unzip.

Forty years later, I still have people come up to me who are now sharing with their own children the four principles I taught them as teenagers! While following those rules may keep people from a physical act of sexual immorality, those rules are incapable of making someone sexually pure—because all immorality begins in the mind.

Just as there is more than one way to murder a person, there is more than one way to commit adultery. Adultery in the bed begins with adultery in the head. That was Jesus's point:

> But I say to you that everyone who looks at a woman with lust for her has already committed adultery with her in his heart. (Matt. 5:28)

Before we go further, let me point out two things Jesus *wasn't* prohibiting. First, Jesus wasn't prohibiting sexual relations within marriage. I know that seems strange to some, but there are some married Christians who believe they are more spiritual if they abstain from sex. In 1 Corinthians 7:3–5, the apostle Paul addressed Christians like that with a simple reply: "Are you out of your mind? Stop robbing your mate and yourself of God's gift!" (my paraphrase). Sex is a gift from God, created and blessed by Him at the beginning of creation (Gen. 1:28).

Second, Jesus wasn't suggesting that it's wrong to look admiringly at another person. He wasn't forbidding natural, normal attraction. That's part of our humanity—it's how God made us. The danger comes when our admiration turns to lust, which is something both men and women can struggle with. Adultery begins with a continued gaze, followed by a mental undressing of the other person and a full-blown imaginary sexual encounter with someone who is not our mate.

Where the scribes and Pharisees had a narrow definition of sexual sin, Jesus had a broad definition of sexual sin. The point of His teaching in Matthew 5:28 is that any sexual activity that is immoral in the bed is also immoral in the head.

In His sermon, Jesus started with the eyes and ended with the heart. Jewish rabbis had a saying: "Eye and heart are the two handmaids of sin."[3] But it's not merely a look that leads to sin; it's a certain kind of look, a lustful look. If we're not careful, looking can slip into lusting. That's what happened to King David in the Old Testament. When David first noticed Bathsheba's beauty, he didn't sin. The sin came when his look lingered and he allowed her beauty to excite his lust. It's not the first glance that causes us to stumble into lust; it's the second glance that lingers and longs for something forbidden.

There's a phrase people today use when describing somebody's attractiveness: *eye candy*. The danger with this phrase is that it affects our perception of the person we are looking at, as if that person is something to be unwrapped and tasted for our enjoyment. And that's what Jesus warned against—seeing another person as an object, a delectable sweet to consume. If we fail to heed His warning, we are rightfully called adulterers, because sexual sins in *fact* are always preceded by sexual sins in *fantasy*. And all who engage in such fantasies are guilty before God.

This brings up a question I am often asked as a pastor: Does marital infidelity mean we can or should get divorced?

A Radical Call to Marital Fidelity

I realize modern marriages are often a complex maze of feelings, responsibilities, and history. As such, teaching on the subject of divorce is like touching a live wire. Many teachers avoid it so they don't get electrocuted. But if you know anything about Jesus, you know He didn't do that—which means neither can we.

He addressed the issue of divorce head-on:

> It was said, "Whoever sends his wife away, let him give her a certificate of divorce"; but I say to you that everyone who divorces his wife, except for the reason of unchastity, makes her commit adultery; and whoever marries a divorced woman commits adultery. (Matt. 5:31–32)

Jesus's illustration about divorce naturally followed His previous illustration because adultery was, and is, one of the leading causes of divorce. When He addressed adultery, Jesus called us to a life of purity. When He addressed divorce, He called us to a life of faithfulness.

Let me point out a couple of things before getting to the heart of Jesus's teaching about divorce. First, there is perhaps no unhappiness more distressing than an unhappy marriage and nothing more tragic than the disintegration of a union God meant for a lifetime of love and fulfillment. David Brooks, a *New York Times* opinion columnist, experienced this unhappiness. He wrote, "There is no loneliness so lonely as the loneliness you feel when you are lying there loveless in bed with another. People go into marriages imagining they are going to sail the open seas together, but when you are in a bad marriage . . . you are trapped in an enclosed basin."[4]

I realize some of you can relate to Brooks, either having lived through an unhappy marriage or being currently in the midst of one. You might be feeling a bit defensive right now. But even if you have divorced and remarried for other than biblical reasons, you can be forgiven by God for that transgression. Admit that mistake to God, and then seek to be the best husband or wife you can in your current relationship. The purpose of this chapter is not to heap a pile of guilt upon you, so I'll strive to be sensitive in handling this topic. But I'll tell you the truth, as Jesus does.

Second, Matthew 5:31–32 doesn't represent everything Jesus has to say on the topic of divorce. In fact, these verses are an abbreviated summary of His teaching. Fortunately, Matthew went on to record Jesus's complete instructions in chapter 19.

To appreciate what Jesus taught about divorce, we need to understand the social and theological controversy swirling around this topic among the Jewish scholars of Jesus's day. This controversy centered on the interpretation of Deuteronomy 24:1, and in particular one word in that verse: "When a man takes a wife and marries her, and it happens that she finds no favor in his eyes because he has found some *indecency* in her, and he writes her a certificate of divorce and puts it in her hand and sends her out from his house."

What does "indecency" mean? The Jews were divided about this. There were two main schools of thought. A popular rabbi named Rabbi Shammai held to the conservative view, and he said you could divorce your wife only for some unspecified sexual sin. However, there was another rabbi, Rabbi Hillel, who held to the liberal view, and he said you could divorce your wife for any reason whatsoever. According to the Jewish historian Josephus, those who were of the Hillel school taught that a man could divorce his wife for any of the following reasons, among many others:

- If she spoiled her husband's dinner with too much salt.
- If she appeared in public with her hair down and her head uncovered.
- If she talked with a nonrelative male in public.
- If she spoke disrespectfully to her husband's parents.[5]

One rabbi who held the liberal view even went so far as to teach that a husband could divorce his wife if he found a more attractive woman and wanted to marry her instead!

It seems unbelievable, but the Pharisees who approached Jesus with a question about divorce held to this liberal position. Matthew 19:3 says, "Some Pharisees came to Jesus, testing Him and asking, 'Is it lawful for a man to divorce his wife for any reason at all?'"[6]

Jesus's answer highlighted three contrasting points of view between Himself and the religious leaders of His day when it came to the question of divorce.[7]

The Pharisees Focused on Divorce, but Jesus Focused on Marriage

The Pharisees asked Jesus a yes or no question, but He didn't give a yes or no answer. Nor did He debate the pros and cons of the various positions on divorce. Instead, Jesus took them back to when God created the institution of marriage, and He asked His own question: "Have you not read that He who created them from the beginning made them male and female, and said, 'For this reason a man shall leave his father and mother and be joined to his wife, and the two shall become one flesh'?" (Matt. 19:4–5).

When we go back to Genesis 1:27 and 2:24, before sin entered the world and ruined everything, we see that God established marriage between one man and one woman for one lifetime. That lifelong union was described with a unique word: "joined" (Gen. 2:24; Matt. 19:5). In Greek, the word is a form of *kollao*, which means "to join closely together, bind closely, unite." Think of it like spiritual Gorilla Glue. The purpose of marriage is to cement two people together for a lifetime.

This binding union is illustrated by the fact that the man and woman become "one flesh," which Jesus highlighted by repeating it in verse 6: "So they are no longer two, but one flesh." Imagine Jesus underlining that phrase "one flesh" and putting an exclamation point next to it. That's the force behind His repetition of the phrase.

The idea of "one flesh" has both a metaphorical and literal meaning. Metaphorically, the man and woman are "joined at the hip," we might say. They complement each other emotionally, mentally, socially, physically, and spiritually. Literally, the man and woman become "one flesh" whenever they come together sexually, which also has the potential of creating a new person, born of their union.

Because of the theological statements from God about marriage in Genesis, Jesus drew the following practical conclusion: "What therefore God has joined together, let no man separate" (Matt. 19:6). I remember years ago going to the drugstore to pick up some photographs I'd left to be developed. Do you remember back when you used to drop off film at a drugstore, and you had to wait a week to go pick up your pictures? When you finally got your photographs, they were in a folder that was held together by sticky glue. I ripped through that folder and reached in for my pictures, but some of the glue had made its way to the pictures and stuck two of them together, front to front. I thought, *How am I going to separate these photographs without destroying them?* Unfortunately, I wasn't successful. When I pulled apart the pictures, it pulled off the faces in both of the photographs as well. That's a good picture of what divorce does. Divorce doesn't just destroy a relationship; it deeply affects the individuals who make up that relationship.

Divorce was not part of God's original design for marriage. Jesus's underlying question to the Pharisees was, "Why are you so focused on divorce when you should be focused on what God intended for marriage?"

The Pharisees Saw a Command, but Jesus Saw a Concession

The Pharisees were bright enough to read between the lines, and they had a ready answer to Jesus's question. They ignored His answer from Genesis and instead took Him back to Deuteronomy 24, asking, "Why then did Moses command to give her a certificate of divorce and send her away?" (Matt. 19:7). You can almost see their smug grins as they thought, *Now we've got Him. How is Jesus going to argue against Moses?* After all, they reasoned, if it were illegal to divorce based on Genesis 2:24, then Moses was breaking God's law by providing for "a certificate of divorce" in Deuteronomy 24:1.

Not so, Jesus said. The Pharisees misunderstood and misapplied Deuteronomy 24:1–4. They placed the importance on the giving of a certificate of divorce and therefore concluded that it was a "command" (Matt. 19:7). However, if you read the passage carefully, in Hebrew, the entire paragraph hinges on a long series of conditional (if) clauses. Divorce could only be granted *if* certain conditions were met. Nowhere did Moses command anyone to divorce. Jesus concluded, "Because of your hardness of heart Moses *permitted* you to divorce your wives; but from the beginning it has not been this way" (v. 8).

Jesus didn't deny that Moses *allowed* a husband to divorce his wife if she met the conditions outlined in Deuteronomy 24, but Jesus did deny that Moses *commanded* a husband to divorce his wife. Divorce is a divine concession because fallen human beings are often hard-hearted.

I remember a wife who had an affair while her husband remained faithful. It started as a long-distance romance—more an emotional attachment than a physical affair. She reconnected with an old boyfriend through Facebook and began a series of late-night phone calls and text messages. Their relationship developed into the exchange of gifts—some of which were inappropriate for him to send to a married woman—and pictures of her wearing his gifts. Her husband discovered her secret affair and confronted her. Her defense was that her husband was emotionally distant and that she was lonely, craving emotional support and affection. Eventually, the emotional affair turned into a physical affair when she traveled to her hometown to visit family.

The husband sought counsel from trusted spiritual advisers who had known the couple for years. They agreed to intervene, speak with her, and see if she would be willing to go to marriage counseling. She didn't want a divorce, since her husband was the sole breadwinner, so she agreed to counseling. But when confronted with the issue of giving up her boyfriend as a concession to work on the marriage, she refused. She wanted her husband's money and her lover's body. As you can imagine, their marriage deteriorated, and they divorced.

Jesus taught there were special circumstances such as adultery that *allowed* the innocent party to divorce, but there were no circumstances that *commanded* a person to divorce.

The Pharisees Were Flippant, but Jesus Was Serious

The Pharisees' question in Matthew 19:7 comes off as flippant, as if marriage and divorce were a matter of curiosity or personal preference. Our own "no-fault" divorce laws enable divorce to be treated lightly by some people. But there are few things more serious than the breakup of a marriage and family.

The Pharisees assumed that a husband could divorce his wife to remarry another woman. Jesus addressed this assumption—and showed how seriously He and God the father took divorce—by saying, "I say to you, whoever divorces his wife, except for immorality, and marries another woman commits adultery" (v. 9). This is the same thing He said in Matthew 5:32. Whereas many of the Pharisees believed a man could divorce his wife for any reason whatsoever, Jesus said only the most serious offense—"immorality"—provided biblical grounds for divorce.

What did Jesus mean by "immorality"? The Greek word for "immorality" is *porneia*, from which we get our word *pornography*. When *porneia* is applied to married people, it refers to any sexual intercourse outside of marriage.

Some people say, "Jesus was talking about unfaithfulness during the engagement period. If your mate is unfaithful while you are engaged, then you can break off the marriage, just as Joseph was tempted to do with Mary." But it's clear Jesus was not talking about the betrothal period; He was talking about marriage. That's what the Pharisees' question was about.

Other people say, "Jesus was talking about an immoral marriage, such as an incestuous marriage or a homosexual marriage." Well, that's ridiculous. Those marriages were forbidden in the Old Testament. They weren't legitimate marriages to begin with. No, "immorality" means what it says. It refers to adultery. According to Jesus, if your mate commits adultery, then you're not commanded to get divorced, but you're allowed to get divorced.

Now, some people say, "Well, you can get divorced, but there's no permission to get remarried." Yes, the Bible gives permission to remarry for two reasons. First of all, Jesus said a person who divorces his wife and "marries another woman" is committing adultery, "except for immorality" (Matt. 19:9). Notice that He included remarriage in that exception. Remember, in Jesus's day, adultery was punishable by death. That means the innocent mate in an adulterous marriage often became a widow, and under the Scriptures, if you're a widow you can get remarried (Rom. 7:2; 1 Cor.

7:39). In other words, just because your adulterous mate in today's society isn't stoned to death doesn't mean you're still bound to him or her after your divorce. You're free to remarry.

Second, it's important to know that the Bible gives one additional allowance for divorce and remarriage, and it's found in 1 Corinthians 7. As Christianity spread like wildfire through the Roman Empire in the decades after Christ, it created some problems that Jesus didn't address. One problem was this: With so many people becoming Christians, what happens if one spouse becomes a Christian but is married to a non-Christian?

In my book *Grace Gone Wild!*, I discuss this situation in detail and give biblical instructions on several scenarios regarding divorce.[8] In short, the apostle Paul affirmed Jesus's teaching about adultery and then gave one more situation in which divorce and remarriage are allowed, and that is *desertion*. If a Christian is deserted by a non-Christian mate, then the Christian is free to remarry. Paul said in 1 Corinthians 7:15, "If the unbelieving one leaves, let him leave; the brother or the sister is not under bondage in such cases." To be "not under bondage" means to be free to remarry.

Now, I want to be very clear: nowhere in Scripture does it say that you have to stay in an abusive situation. If you or your children are being physically abused or threatened by your spouse, God does not require you to live in that situation. The sanctity of life refers to more than just life inside the womb. All life is sacred to God; He hates violence. If you are in an abusive marriage, then you are free under Scripture to get out of that house and protect yourself and your children. But if you end up divorcing because of abuse, the Bible says you must remain unmarried or return to your spouse (1 Cor. 7:10–11). That is how seriously God takes divorce.

A Radical Remedy for Infidelity

How can we live pure lives in such a sensual society—one that celebrates sexual promiscuity, including adultery? Jesus's answer to that question serves as a fitting application for us today:

> If your right eye makes you stumble, tear it out and throw it from you; for it is better for you to lose one of the parts of your body, than for your whole body to be thrown into hell. If your right hand makes you stumble, cut it off and throw it from you; for it is better for you to lose one of the parts of your body, than for your whole body to go into hell. (Matt. 5:29–30)

This is one of Jesus's most demanding statements—and although we shouldn't take it literally, we should take it seriously. Jesus used "eyes" here, because as I mentioned earlier, adultery in the head (enticed by sight) happens before adultery in the bed. Jesus used "hands" because adultery, even mental adultery, is a form of stealing what belongs to another person (sexual intimacy in marriage) for your own perverted ends.

Jesus was saying, "You have to deal decisively with any sin in your life. That means you cut it out, no matter how painful it is." Remember, in Jesus's day, there were no anesthetics. Surgery meant sawing off a hand or gouging out an eye without any relief from pain. But as horrific as that experience is, Jesus said, it would be better to go through that short-term pain than to experience the eternal consequences of hell.

Let me be specific. Are there certain websites, television programs, or movies that incite lust in you? It doesn't matter how much you enjoy them; if they are causing you to think immorally, you need to cut those things out of your life. Are you in a job where something or someone is tempting you toward sin? Jesus was saying it would be better to quit your job than to continue being tempted and fall victim to immorality. No matter how inconvenient it is, you need to deal decisively with that temptation. Is there a relationship you're in right now that you know is dangerous and is leading in a direction you should not go? No matter how painful it is, you need to end that relationship now.

I remember, in a previous church, a man came to see me. He told me about a woman he met at work who was going through a divorce, and he spent his lunch hours counseling her, trying to help her. Those lunchtime counseling sessions turned into phone calls and a deeper relationship, and although the relationship had not yet turned into immorality, it was very close to doing so. This man realized the relationship was having a negative effect on his spiritual life and on his marriage. He asked, "Pastor, what should I do?" I said, "You need to cut off that relationship right now. No more phone calls, no more meetings, no more involvement at all." He started to protest. He said, "That would be too painful. I don't think I could do that. That would hurt me; that would hurt her." I said, "That's all the more reason you need to stop." And then I quoted Proverbs 6:27: "Can a man take fire in his bosom and his clothes not be burned?" If you play with fire long enough, you're going to get burned. And that's why Jesus said if there is any immoral activity, or even close to immoral activity, in your life, it is time to cut it off. Better to do that than to lose your eternal soul.

All adultery, whether in fact or fantasy, is outside the bounds of God's design for human sexual relations and is therefore sinful. Jesus said to get rid of anything that "makes you stumble." Literally, the word Jesus used here means "stumbling block." It's like a LEGO brick you step on barefooted in the middle of the night. Jesus said to get rid of those things and be ruthless about it. Take whatever drastic measures are necessary to protect your spiritual health.

How to Keep from Stumbling

For too long, believers have flirted with sin. But God's Word is clear: we are to "flee from sexual immorality" (1 Cor. 6:18 NIV). We are to hate sin and to root it out of every nook and cranny of our lives. In Colossians 3:5, the apostle Paul said, "Put to death, therefore, whatever belongs to your earthly nature: sexual immorality, impurity, lust, evil desires and greed, which is idolatry" (NIV), because these things lead to "the wrath of God" (v. 6)—just as Jesus described in Matthew 5.

So how do we do this? How do we keep from stumbling into adultery of the mind or body, which could destroy our marriages and families? Let me offer two practical suggestions.

First, *develop a contract with your eyes*. Job said, "I have made a covenant with my eyes; how then could I gaze at a virgin?" (31:1). Then he added, "If my step has turned from the way, or my heart followed my eyes . . . let my crops be uprooted. If my heart has been enticed by a woman . . . that would be a lustful crime; moreover, it would be an iniquity punishable by judges" (vv. 7–9, 11).

If you want to be a godly person, then follow Job's example: never take a second glance, and when speaking with somebody of the opposite sex, don't have a wandering, lingering gaze, consuming that person as an attractive object of desire. Godly people place guards over their eyes when it comes to watching television and movies, reading books and magazines, and scrolling social media and the internet.

Second, *determine to think differently.* We must resist the pull to conform to sinful ways by choosing to transform our minds. The apostle Paul said in Romans 12:2, "Do not be conformed to this world, but be transformed by the renewing of your mind, so that you may prove what the will of God is, that which is good and acceptable and perfect." How do you transform your mind? By thinking on things that are pure—or, as Paul put it, "that which is good and acceptable and perfect." Paul expanded on this theme in Philippians 4:8: "Finally, brethren, whatever is true, whatever is honorable, whatever is right, whatever is pure, whatever is lovely, whatever is of good repute, if there is any excellence and if anything worthy of praise, dwell on these things."

This reminds me of a scene from the Disney movie *Peter Pan,* which my triplet grandchildren love! When I took my grandchildren to Disneyland to ride the Peter Pan ride recently, I thought of the scene in which Peter Pan told the children that, to get to Neverland, they should simply fly. But the children didn't know how. So Peter instructed them, "Now, think of the happiest things. It's the same as having wings!"[9] That may or may not work for flying, but it absolutely works for driving out immoral thoughts from our minds.

I could summarize these two points like this: *don't linger in your look* and *don't conform but transform your thinking*. If you practice these two ideas daily, even hourly, then you have a chance to keep from stumbling into adultery.

But if you do stumble, remember this: adultery is not un-forgiveable. Adultery is a terrible sin, but it is one covered by the blood of Christ and the grace of God if you repent and ask for forgiveness. No, God's grace does not automatically erase the temporary—even lifelong—consequences you may experience for your sin, but His grace does erase the *eternal* consequences of your sin. If you sincerely ask, God will grant you a pardon from an eternal separation from Him in hell. But He will also tell you, "Go, and sin no more" (John 8:11 KJV).

five

Straight Talk about
Your Adversaries

BY THE TIME GEORG KILLED THE MAN who killed his brother, the vendetta that had engulfed his family had taken the lives of forty-four people. Georg knew he would be the next to die.

This is the plot of the novel *Broken April* by Ismail Kadare.[1] In the highlands of Albania, Georg is caught in a multigenerational killing spree with a rival family. The feud began long before Georg was born, when a stranger passed by Georg's grandfather's home one evening. Custom dictated that his grandfather welcome the stranger into his home and offer him food and shelter. The next morning, Georg's grandfather escorted the stranger to the edge of the village. Just as the grandfather turned to go, a shot rang out. The stranger had been involved in a feud of his own and had now been killed. He fell facedown toward the village, which meant the stranger was technically still a guest of Georg's grandfather and under his protection. By the codes of hospitality and honor, the grandfather and his family were bound to avenge this man's death by killing a member of the shooter's family.

Ironically, had the man fallen away from the village, neither Georg's grandfather nor the rest of the family would have been obliged to avenge the man's death. But as it was, the family was thrown into a seventy-year feud with another family they knew nothing about.

Georg and his family were engaged in one of the oldest practices in human history: revenge and retaliation. In their culture, honor demanded payback, not unlike the retaliation that happens among gangs or the Mafia. Vendettas lead to ever-escalating vengeance and violence. This is illustrated well in the movie *The Untouchables*, where Sean Connery played a tough Irish-American cop in 1930s Chicago. He joined a special task force headed by FBI agent Eliot Ness, portrayed by Kevin Costner. The two men were tasked with rooting out Al Capone's mob syndicate, which was running bootlegged alcohol across the border from Canada. During one climactic scene, Connery's character said to Ness, "You wanna get Capone? Here's how you get him. He pulls a knife; you pull a gun. He sends one of yours to the hospital; you send one of his to the morgue. *That's* the Chicago way!"[2]

The cold dish of revenge is one many of us have savored. We've lain in bed at night dreaming of ways to get back at someone who wronged us or thinking of comebacks we wish we'd said at the time. Even if we haven't gone as far as Georg in exacting our pound of flesh, many of us have retaliated in some measure—at least in our hearts. But Jesus said, "Don't go there. Even revenge in the heart is a step in the wrong direction."

In Matthew 5:38–48, the Lord wrapped up this section of His talk with two final illustrations of what it means to surpass the righteousness of the scribes and Pharisees (v. 20).[3] As with His other examples, Jesus was calling His followers to radical righteousness—to conform our character and conduct to God's standards.

Both of Jesus's illustrations in this passage answer the same question: How should we treat our enemies? His first illustration challenges us to release rather than retaliate (vv. 38–42). His second example challenges us to love rather than hate (vv. 43–47). Jesus then concluded with a summary statement that is the central theme of His sermon: "Therefore you are to be perfect, as your heavenly Father is perfect" (v. 48)—a goal that seems impossible unless properly understood.

Release, Don't Retaliate

Whenever we've been treated unfairly or our rights have been violated, we naturally want to seek revenge. In many cases, if we could get away with it, we'd like to wring the neck of the person who wronged us. We may couch our desire for retaliation in cute phrases like, "Don't get mad. Get even." But the philosophy is the same. Don't let anybody run over you. Stand up for your rights. Mark your boundaries. Don't let anybody get the best of you.

Jesus addressed that desire next in His sermon. He said that if you're a Christian, you're going to have a radically different response to wrongdoing.

Rights and Retaliation

From our earliest days in school, Americans learn that we have "unalienable" rights conferred by our Creator, including "life, liberty and the pursuit of happiness."[4] These and other rights are secured in our Constitution and Bill of Rights: the right to exercise our faith in public and private, to speak our minds, to assemble, and to petition the government, for example. Because America was founded to protect our God-given rights, the phrase "I have my rights" is a common refrain on many American tongues.

Some of our most valued rights concern our justice system. No one from the government can kick in our door and seize our personal property or our person without a warrant. If we are arrested and placed on trial, judgment will come from a jury of our fellow citizens. And if we are found guilty, the punishment will be equal to the crime. This last point comes from one of the most ancient laws in human history.[5] Jesus quoted it in Matthew 5:38:

> You have heard that it was said, "An eye for an eye, and a tooth for a tooth."

The idea of a law limiting punishment on the guilty was first written in the Code of Hammurabi, who ruled over Babylon during the time of the Old Testament patriarchs Abraham, Isaac, and Jacob. It read in part, "If a man has caused the loss of a gentleman's eye, his eye one shall cause to be lost. If he has shattered a gentleman's limb, one shall shatter his limb. . . . If he has made the tooth of a man . . . fall out, one shall make his tooth fall out."[6]

Moses simplified the law, saying, "Eye for eye, tooth for tooth" (Exod. 21:24). In Latin, this law is known as *lex talionis*—the law of retaliation. It was the law practiced by Georg in Kadare's novel and advocated by Sean Connery's character in *The Untouchables*. It's a law practiced today by street gangs and drug cartels—and to a lesser extent by many of us whenever we get back at someone. It was a law my brother and I practiced on each other growing up. If he locked me out of the bathroom, I'd pour a vial of liquid that smelled like cat urine on his pillow. He'd retaliate, and I'd seek my revenge. And so it went—tit for tat, eye for eye, tooth for tooth.

The Old Testament civil law was given to prevent judges and courts from handing down excessive sentences. The purpose of the law was to establish a foundation of justice by specifying the punishment a wrongdoer deserved and limiting the compensation a victim deserved to an equivalent amount and no more. The beauty in the law is that it provided a clear definition of justice—if you violated the law, then justice would come upon you in equal measure. Plus, it restrained revenge or taking the law into one's own hands.

Let me say this very clearly: you *do* have rights conferred upon you by your Creator. And when those rights are violated, you have a right to seek justice. The reason we human beings crave justice is that we were created in the image of God, who seeks justice. God never asks you to give up your right to justice. But as followers of Jesus Christ, when we are wronged, we are to release our desire for *retaliation*.

The word *retaliation* is another word for *vengeance*—our attempt to settle the score ourselves, to hurt someone else for hurting us. The apostle Paul wrote in Romans 12:19–20: "Never take your own revenge, beloved, but leave room for the wrath of God, for it is written, 'Vengeance is Mine, I will repay,' says the Lord."

We are to surrender our desire for vengeance (or retaliation), but never are we asked to surrender our desire for justice when our real rights are violated. There is nothing wrong with desiring someone who has wronged us to suffer the consequences of the offense. But a desire for justice means letting God or someone else settle the score for us. In fact, Paul continued his discussion of vengeance in Romans 13 by declaring that government was a "minister of God, an avenger who brings wrath on the one who practices evil" (v. 4).

You've probably heard the saying, "We are a nation of laws, not of men." We don't allow for vigilantism in our culture. If somebody harms your family, you can defend yourself, but you can't seek vengeance—you don't go after them with a shotgun and take justice into your own hands. It's just not right to do that. And this was true in Jesus's day as well. Rome was a nation of laws. They did not allow for retaliation. You had to turn it over to the government.

However, the scribes and Pharisees took the Old Testament law that was intended to regulate justice in the courts (where it belonged) and applied it to personal relationships (where it didn't belong). They used the law to settle disputes among family members, friends, neighbors, coworkers, and strangers. According to the Pharisees, the Old Testament gave permission for anyone to become judge, jury, and executioner when wronged, even though the Lord explicitly forbade personal vengeance, saying, "You shall not take vengeance, nor bear any grudge against the sons of your people" (Lev. 19:18).

Release Your Rights

In the Sermon on the Mount, Jesus picked up on the idea of not seeking your own vengeance, and He pushed it to a radical conclusion. In Matthew 5:39, Jesus said, "I say to you, do not resist an evil person."

I can hear the brakes in your mind squealing as your thoughts come to a halt. *Wait a minute. Did Jesus really say, "Do not resist an evil person"? Not ever?* Now, Jesus was speaking in hyperbole here. He wasn't saying don't ever defend yourself. What He was saying is that sometimes the only way to break the cycle of anger and violence is to choose not to retaliate against evil.

Before I go any further, I know you probably have some objections to this idea of releasing your desire for retaliation against those who are hurting you. I know I did when I read the passage. Some people say, "This is an impractical command, not to resist an evil person. That's a sweet Sunday school sentiment, but it doesn't work in the real world." The reason people feel that way is they have tried to apply this passage to situations in which God never intended it to be applied. For example, some people use this passage in defense of pacifism as a national policy. They say, "Jesus meant that if somebody drops a bomb on our country, then we need to send a bouquet of flowers in return." No, that's not what the Bible is saying. This passage doesn't deal with nations; it's talking about individuals.

Other people mistakenly apply this verse to physical abuse. They say, "If your mate is physically abusing you or your children, then you have to stay in that relationship. You are not allowed to defend yourself." No! As we saw in the previous chapter, the Bible *never* calls for anyone to jeopardize their physical safety—or the safety of someone they are responsible for—when they have the ability to remove themselves or their loved ones from that situation. All life is sacred, and God hates violence. In fact, the primary reason God gave for destroying the world by a flood was the physical violence in the world (Gen. 6:13). No, this teaching from Jesus applies specifically to the area of personal offenses. He was describing how Christians are to respond when they are personally wronged.

In Matthew 5:39–42, Jesus gave four illustrations that show the lengths to which truly righteous people will go to hold their personal rights loosely:

> But I say to you, do not resist an evil person; but whoever slaps you on your right cheek, turn the other to him also. If anyone wants to sue you and take your shirt, let him have your coat also. Whoever forces you to go one mile, go with him two. Give to him who asks of you, and do not turn away from him who wants to borrow from you.

In each of these examples, an "evil person" seeks to do us harm. First, a person insults us. Then somebody sues us for our rightful property. Next, somebody forces us to do something against our will. Finally, somebody begs for money from us. In each of these examples, our rights have been violated, but we are to release and not retaliate.

First, we *release our right to dignity*. Jesus said, "Whoever slaps you on your right cheek, turn the other to him also" (v. 39). Jesus wasn't talking about a fist to your face or an open-palmed smack where someone might leave a handprint on your cheek. Rather, the idea is a backhanded slap. The early rabbis taught that hitting someone with the back of the hand was twice as insulting as hitting someone square in the jaw. It was a form of contempt because it declared the person wasn't worth the effort of a real blow.

The backhanded slap is meant to be an insult more than an injury. For example, we might say today, "That was a backhanded compliment," which means it wasn't a compliment but an insult. So what Jesus was driving at isn't physical assault but verbal assault, which hits like a slap in the face.

This reminds me of the patron saint of British insulters, Winston Churchill. One day, Churchill received an invitation from playwright George Bernard Shaw to attend the premiere of a play. "Am reserving two tickets for you, for my premiere. Come and bring a friend—if you have one," Shaw wrote. Churchill responded with a regret: "Impossible to be present for the first performance. Will attend second—if there is one."[7]

Our rights and the law of *lex talionis*, if applied personally, tell us to let the zingers fly. Respond to every insult with a better insult. But Jesus said to get rid of our petty plans of revenge. For example, if your spouse is messy, don't make a bigger mess to teach them a lesson. If your friend is late for lunch, don't make it a point to be later the next time. If a coworker makes a cutting remark out of frustration, don't blast that person on social media.

That goes against our natural grain, doesn't it? If somebody insults us, even in fun, what is our first thought? *Man, I've got to have a quick comeback to this.* Not long ago, a religious leader published an open letter to me, criticizing me for something I'd said on television. Driving home from work the day I read the letter, I came up with the best one-liner to send back to him. It was absolutely perfect—in one sentence, I could have cut him to shreds. I got so excited thinking about sending that comeback to the press, then I remembered this passage. I realized, *I can't send that email with a clear conscience.* So I didn't do it. But that's the natural response we all have, isn't it? If somebody takes a swing at us, we want to swing back. But Jesus said don't do it. He said to turn the other cheek and make the well-being of the other person our focus, to release our right to dignity and make the other person's dignity paramount by refusing to retaliate.

Second, we *release our right to property.* Jesus said, "If anyone wants to sue you and take your shirt, let him have your coat also" (v. 40). In Jesus's day, someone's "coat," or cloak, was viewed as an almost inalienable right. Virtually any possession could be taken from somebody, but not a person's coat, not permanently. Days in Israel can be hot, but nights are almost always cool. For many people in the first century, their only means of warmth was a full-length cloak also used as a blanket. So if someone sued you and won the shirt off your back and your cloak as well, the winner of the lawsuit had to allow you to use the cloak at night (Exod. 22:26–27; Deut. 24:13).

Our right to our own property compels us to fight for what is ours. And that isn't always the wrong thing to do. There is no biblical command never to go to court for any reason when being taken advantage of. Even Jesus talked about a widow who went to a judge to seek relief when she was being exploited by those who wanted to steal her property (Luke 18:1–8). God often executes justice through the legal system. But what Jesus was condemning was an attitude so focused on protecting our property—or other rights—that we lose sight of our responsibility to others. In this illustration, Jesus advocated generosity, even toward those who have wronged us.

When we speak of a generous person, we say, "He'd give you the shirt off his back." Jesus was saying, "Great. But the really generous person—the one who represents a righteousness that surpasses the scribes and Pharisees—also gives away his coat."

Look again at Romans 12:19–20, in which Paul picked up this point when he wrote, "Never take your own revenge, beloved, but leave room for the wrath of God, for it is written, 'Vengeance is Mine, I will repay,' says the Lord. 'But if your enemy is hungry, feed him, and if he is thirsty, give him a drink; for in so doing you will heap burning coals on his head.'"

What did Paul mean by, "leave room for the wrath of God"? When you are wronged, you can either try to settle the score yourself, or you can let God do so. If you want to be the one to try to square accounts with your enemy, then God says, "Fine; I'll sit on the sidelines and let you try to do it. But guess what? I'm much better at it than you are." God has a way of evening the score much more efficiently than we can. And when God does it, He does it in a redemptive way. Yes, He brings justice, but He also tries to bring redemption to the person who has wronged us. That's why it's so important that we not take vengeance ourselves.

Releasing your rights means to do good for those who oppose you. And by doing so, Paul said, you "heap burning coals on his head"—that is, you give your adversary the conviction of wrong in the hopes of bringing that person to repentance. Revenge never leads to repentance, but being generous with your property—whether a coat, a hot meal, or a cool drink—just might turn enmity into amity.

Third, Jesus encourages us to *release our right to autonomy*. This is where we get the expression "Go the extra mile." Jesus said, "Whoever forces you to go one mile, go with him two" (Matt. 5:41). In the Roman-occupied Israel of Jesus's day, a Roman soldier had the authority to compel Jewish citizens to carry the soldier's luggage. However, a soldier couldn't force anyone to carry anything for more than one mile.

Imagine how angry you'd be if you were walking down the street, minding your own business, when a Roman soldier called you over and told you to pick up his bag and carry it in the opposite direction. Proud Jews despised having to stoop so low. It wasn't enough that these pagans occupied their country; now they could demand that people alter their plans for the day and go somewhere they'd rather not go. It was an affront to the Jews' sense of autonomy—their personal independence and right to make up their own minds about whether they wanted to travel east or west, north or south, or not at all.

Whenever someone encroaches on our sense of autonomy, we naturally resent it. But Jesus said, "Let go of all that. In fact, not only go the first mile with a good attitude, but throw in an extra mile for free. Who knows? Maybe the one pushing you around will stop and wonder what's gotten into you. Then you can tell that person about Me." I think that's what is behind Jesus's statement in verse 41. If you've been asked to wash the dishes, then dry them and put them in the cabinet too. If you're told to mow the lawn, then edge it and blow off the grass too. If the boss tells you to work late to finish the project, then buy pizza for everyone else too. Go the extra mile.

Fourth, we *release our right to money*. Up until this point we might say Jesus was merely preaching, but now He's meddling. He said, "Give to him who asks of you, and do not turn away from him who wants to borrow from you" (v. 42).

Jesus wasn't saying to give away what you don't have. The assumption is that you have the means to give. Jesus also wasn't saying to give everything you own until you become destitute. Nor was He saying to give indiscriminately, like throwing money in the air on a busy street. What Jesus *was* saying is if you have something others can use, even if they are on the other side of the fence, give it, especially if they ask for it. For example, if you own a pickup truck, you probably never knew how many friends you had until you bought that truck!

Will you get ripped off? Probably. Will others take advantage of you? Sure. All the generous people I know have had the wool pulled over their eyes. When I was in college, I used to make extra money playing my accordion for bar mitzvahs, weddings, and other engagements. One day, I got a telephone call from a bandleader in Fort Worth. He said, "We'd like you to come and play for a wedding reception. If you'll play the whole evening, we'll give you sixty-five dollars." To me, that was a small fortune! So I drove to Fort Worth and spent Saturday night playing at the wedding. When the wedding was over, the bandleader said, "I'm sorry, Robert. I don't have the cash with me, but I'll send you a check." I fell for it. Every day for the next two weeks, I went to the mailbox looking for that check. As each day came and went with no check, I became pretty steamed. Finally, I called the bandleader. He didn't even pretend he was going to pay me. He called me an unspeakable name, and I responded in turn with an expletive I had never used before and have never used since. In the end, my desire for sixty-five dollars cost me two weeks of my life, not to mention my verbal virginity. I was in emotional bondage to that guy because he owed me a debt. I could go no further while I was waiting on that check. Choosing to release a debt, whether it's a financial or an emotional one, is many times the only way we can be free to get on with our lives.

When we've been wronged, Jesus wants us to take seriously His command in Luke 6:35: "Love your enemies, and do good, and lend, expecting nothing in return." Then trust the Lord to balance the accounts as He sees fit. So for whom can you do something good today? Do you know someone in financial need? What have you given to help that person? Why don't you open your wallet and do good for someone, without expecting something in return?

Be an Anvil, Not a Doormat

Jesus knew these commands would hit us like a shock to the heart. He also knew that following His commands would shock our adversaries, disarming them and reducing the heat so we might be reconciled.

Some read Jesus's words in Matthew 5:38–42 and conclude He was advocating a weak-kneed timidity when it comes to personal abuse. Nonsense! The Lord mentioned being slapped on the cheek only twice, not a dozen times.

We're not to let others walk all over us. Charles Spurgeon said we "are to be the anvil when bad men are the hammer."[8] An anvil is not a doormat. It's important to remember, as I said earlier, that nowhere in Scripture are we instructed to be victims of abuse, rape, theft, or murder. Nor are we to stand by idly while others are assaulted. Valuing the sanctity of life means valuing the lives of others *and* ourselves.

There is nothing noble or in keeping with the spirit of Jesus to watch a bully assault someone on the street or allow someone to break into your home and carry off your valuables. But it is noble and in keeping with the spirit of Jesus's instruction to bite your tongue when someone insults you at the grocery store or to refuse to lean on your horn when someone cuts you off on the freeway or to keep quiet when someone berates you for your parenting choices.

Be an anvil, not a doormat.

Love, Don't Hate

Jesus wasn't quite finished with His followers yet. He had one more thing to say about how we are to surpass the righteousness of the scribes and Pharisees: we are to love better than they do:

> You have heard that it was said, "You shall love your neighbor and hate your enemy." (Matt. 5:43)

Jesus's audience was taught, "You shall love your neighbor and hate your enemy" (v. 43). The command to love comes from Leviticus 19:18, but there is no command to hate in Scripture. According to the Pharisees, the opposite of love was hate, and the opposite of a neighbor was anyone unneighborly—namely, anyone who wasn't part of your family, race, and religion.

Not according to Jesus. He continued,

But I say to you, love your enemies and pray for those who persecute you. (v. 44)

Love is the great cleansing agent; it cuts through the grime of our adversary's hateful attitudes and actions toward us so we can see what lies beneath. Love allows us to look into the soul of a person and see hurt, disappointment, guilt, and shame. Love motivates us to pray for those who mistreat us so they might know the grace and mercy of God.

A wonderful example of this kind of love comes from Corrie ten Boom. In 1947, having been freed from a Nazi concentration camp only a couple of years earlier, Corrie traveled from her home in Holland to Munich, Germany, to bring the message of God's love and forgiveness. After she spoke, a balding, heavyset man in a gray overcoat approached her. She later wrote, "One moment I saw the overcoat and the brown hat; the next, a blue uniform and a visored cap with its skull and crossbones." He had been a guard at Ravensbrück, the concentration camp where Corrie and her sister, Betsie, had been imprisoned.

"A fine message, *fräulein*! How good it is to know that, as you say, all our sins are at the bottom of the sea!" he said with his hand extended. "You mentioned Ravensbrück in your talk. I was a guard in there. But since that time, I have become a Christian. I know that God has forgiven me for the cruel things I did there, but I would like to hear it from your lips as well. *Fräulein*, will you forgive me?"

His hand remained extended, and Corrie wrestled with herself. Should she take his hand and offer him forgiveness? She prayed for God's help. Then, she wrote, "Woodenly, mechanically, I thrust my hand into the one stretched out to me. And as I did, an incredible thing took place. . . . This healing warmth seemed to flood my whole being, bringing tears to my eyes. 'I forgive you, brother!' I cried. 'With all my heart!' For a long moment we grasped each other's hands, the former guard and the former prisoner. I had never known God's love so intensely as I did then."[9]

Love Makes Us Like God

To love and pray for our enemies is to be like Christ, who prayed for His executioners as they drove nails into His hands and feet, "Father, forgive them; for they do not know what they are doing" (Luke 23:34). Jesus said when we love and pray for our adversaries, we also represent the character of God:

> Love your enemies and pray for those who persecute you, so that you may be sons [and daughters] of your Father who is in heaven; for He causes His sun to rise on the evil and the good, and sends rain on the righteous and the unrighteous. (Matt. 5:44–45)

God's love is available to everyone. A rainstorm after a drought blesses the godly and the ungodly alike. The vitamin D we get from the sun is beneficial to the vilest pagan and the holiest person we know. That's love. And to love as God loves is to be like God.

You likely know somebody in your circle who is hard to love. Who is that person? Make it your determined mission to pray for that person. But prayer is just one expression of love. What else can you do for that person; what little graces can you perform for him or her, just as God brings rain and sunshine to all?

Love Makes Us Different from the World

Jesus drove home the idea of loving our adversaries by pointing out that this kind of love makes us different from everyone else in the world. It's easy to love our family and friends. But Jesus asked,

> If you love those who love you, what reward do you have? Do not even the tax collectors do the same? (Matt. 5:46)

In that time and place, tax collectors were despised. They were local Jews who worked with the Roman government to collect payment from their fellow citizens. Often unscrupulous, they collected more money than was necessary and pocketed the excess. Everyone hated tax collectors, except other tax collectors. But to love them as Jesus did, well, that would make us different—radically so.

Here's another example of a loving action that makes us distinct from the culture. Jesus said,

> If you greet only your brothers, what more are you doing than others? Do not even the Gentiles do the same? (v. 47)

In Jesus's day, Jews looked down on non-Jews (Gentiles) and considered them as little better than mangy, flea-ridden dogs. But even dogs bark to one another in greeting. As followers of Christ, we're to do more than what everyone else does—to love more, to show more respect and courtesy. If we can't or won't, then we're no different from the average Joe or Jane walking down the street; we certainly don't reflect the image of God.

To love and greet only your family or tribe is natural—every wicked person does that. What isn't natural is to love and greet outsiders, especially if they are considered enemies. Jesus called us to exceed the righteousness of the Pharisees and love more than the pagans. That love is supernatural and requires the Holy Spirit to mold our character and conduct until we reflect the character and conduct of God.

So what are you doing to surrender your life to the work of the Spirit? Do you spend concentrated time in God's Word, thinking about how to apply it to your life? Are you asking God to shape your attitudes so your actions demonstrate the love Jesus was talking about? Do you have a trusted friend who can tell you hard things about yourself and point you to Christ? If not, you need to find one.

Perfection, Not Imperfection

The "therefore" in Matthew 5:48 indicates that Jesus is about to summarize what it means to surpass the righteousness of the scribes and Pharisees (v. 20), as well as the Old Testament illustrations found in verses 21–47. He said,

> Therefore you are to be perfect, as your heavenly Father is perfect. (v. 48)

117

God told the Israelites to be holy because He is holy (Lev. 19:2), and the apostle John said to love because God is love (1 John 4:7–8). Jesus told us to be perfect because God is perfect.

The standard is God—and God alone. That's what it means to be righteous, or "perfect"—to conform our character and conduct to God's standard when it comes to releasing hatred in our hearts, being faithful in marriage, refusing to retaliate, and loving our enemies. Achieving perfect righteousness is impossible this side of heaven, yet Jesus still calls us to pursue it. And in that pursuit, we pursue God Himself.

Maybe, since you've been reading this chapter, God has brought to your mind somebody who has wronged you, somebody who has hurt you deeply. Maybe you're tired of carrying that bitterness around in your heart; maybe you're tired of wondering and worrying about what that person is going to do to you next. Are you ready to let go of that? Jesus wants His followers to release, not retaliate. To love, not hate. Booker T. Washington once said, "I would permit no man . . . to narrow and degrade my soul by making me hate him."[10] Perhaps the best thing you can do is to pray for God's best in that person's life.

Gandhi reportedly said that if we practiced the law of retaliation endlessly—an eye for an eye and a tooth for a tooth—then the whole world would be blind and toothless. Jesus offers a better way—a demanding way, but, nevertheless, a better way.

A reliable scholar from many years ago, Alfred Plummer, concluded his commentary on this section of the Sermon on the Mount with words I find fitting: "To return evil for good is devilish; to return good for good is human; to return good for evil is divine. To love as God loves is moral perfection and this perfection Christ tells us to aim at."[11]

Aim high, hit high. Aim at God, and you will find your character and conduct slowly taking on a Christlike quality. Nothing would surpass the righteousness of the world's scribes and Pharisees more than that.

six

Straight Talk about Your Church

A FATHER TOOK HIS SON TO CHURCH because he wanted his boy to know about the love and grace of Jesus. However, when they arrived at the service and sat down in the pew, the one squirming wasn't the little boy; it was the father. He was impatient for the service to start. During the service, the father grumbled that he didn't like the songs they sang, the soloist was off-key, and the sermon was too long.

Once church was over, the father said a cuss word or two about the heat and the traffic as he drove to a restaurant for lunch. When they arrived at the restaurant, he fussed about how slow the server was in taking their order. And when his meal arrived, he fumed that the server got his order wrong. Once his order was corrected, he turned to his son and said, "Bow your head, son, so we can thank God." His son bowed his head and listened to his father pray: "Heavenly Father, we thank You for the service this morning at church. We thank You for our pastor. Bless him. Thank You, Father, for this meal. Bless those who prepared and served it. Please use it to strengthen our bodies that we might continue to serve You and be a blessing to others. Amen."

The little boy said "Amen" too. But before diving into his French fries, he asked, "Daddy, did God hear you at church when you fussed about the hymns and the woman who sang and the preacher?"

The father, a little embarrassed, said, "Well, yes, son, God heard me."

"And," the boy continued, "did God hear you when you cussed in the car?"

The father, now more than a little bit embarrassed, said, "I shouldn't have said those words, but yes, I suppose God heard me."

"And when you complained about the man who brought us our lunch?"

"Yes, God heard me then too. Eat your hamburger."

The boy picked up a fry and put it in his mouth and chewed. "Daddy, did God hear you when you prayed for the food?"

"Yes, son. God hears all our prayers."

The boy thought for a moment and then asked his father, "If God heard everything you said, then which one did He believe?"

Ouch!

There are two people you can never fool: God, who knows everything, and a child who isn't afraid to call out your hypocrisy.

Journalist Ambrose Bierce once described a hypocrite as "one who, professing virtues that he does not respect, secures the advantage of seeming to be what he despises."[1] In other words, a hypocrite is someone who pretends to be one thing but in reality is another thing. Uncovering someone's hypocrisy is disconcerting, whether the person is a believer or not. But hypocrisy in the life of a Christian carries potentially devastating consequences.

Throughout the Sermon on the Mount, Jesus talked about the authentic articles of our faith. He began His hillside talk with the Beatitudes, laying out the essential qualities of Christian character. He went on to explain that when we put this character into practice, we can influence our culture as light penetrates darkness and salt penetrates meat. He then helped us understand authentic righteousness by correcting misinterpretations about the Old Testament regarding our actions and our attitudes. Next, in Matthew 6:1–18, Jesus tackled the sin of hypocrisy by correcting misconceptions about how we are to practice our righteousness at church and during religious activities.

Beware of Hypocrisy

Few things churned Jesus's stomach more than people strutting their spirituality in public. Perhaps that's why He reserved His harshest criticism for those who liked to show off their piousness for the sole purpose of impressing others. He denounced the religious leaders of His day, saying, "This people honors Me with their lips, but their heart is far away from Me" (Matt. 15:8).

Jesus saw what was in the hearts of these religious leaders. Sure, they had a veneer of religiosity about them, but their hearts were far from God. I remember my mom used to say, "The one thing people will never forgive you for is being able to see through them." That's true. Jesus could see right through those Pharisees. That's why He repeatedly pronounced "woe"—an exclamation of divine judgment—on the scribes and Pharisees, calling them "hypocrites" (23:13–39).

Hypocrisy isn't something to play around with. In fact, Jesus told us to "beware of practicing your righteousness before men to be noticed by them" (6:1)—that is, to be thought of by others as superspiritual.

The Dangers of Hypocrisy

The word *hypocrite* comes from the Greek *hypokrites* and basically means "to wear a mask." It refers to Greek actors who would put on a mask in order to pretend to be somebody they actually weren't. Hypocrites are two-faced; they say one thing but live in a completely different way.

Hypocrites come in two varieties: those who *knowingly* act a part and deceive others, and those who *unknowingly* act a part and deceive only themselves. In either case, Jesus warned us that hypocrisy is a hideous spiritual disease. Just as cancer wreaks havoc in our bodies, so hypocrisy, if it metastasizes and isn't cut out, wreaks havoc in the body of Christ—the church. It works like this:

- First, *hypocrisy distorts the truth*. Like standing in front of a fun-house mirror, where you sort of recognize yourself but everything is either elongated or squished out of proportion, so the truth becomes distorted and harder to recognize.
- Then, with the truth out of focus, *hypocrisy causes confusion*. Like the little boy in the story at the

beginning of this chapter, we aren't sure what God thinks is right or wrong.

- Finally, when the truth is distorted and people are confused (including ourselves), *hypocrisy leads us to believe lies and disbelieve truth*.

This last point plays itself out in the church by causing divisions, which the Lord hates (Prov. 6:16, 19). Paul warned the Christians in Rome to have nothing to do with those "who cause dissensions and hindrances contrary to the teaching which you learned" (Rom. 16:17). In fact, his admonition to Titus was even stronger: "If people are causing divisions among you, give a first and second warning. After that, have nothing more to do with them. For people like that have turned away from the truth, and their own sins condemn them" (Titus 3:10–11 NLT).

One way these divisions played out in the early church, and in our churches today as well, was by pitting one preacher against another. For example, people often tell me who their favorite preachers are—David Jeremiah, Chuck Swindoll, Charles Stanley, and so on—and then they obligingly add as an afterthought, "And of course, you, Dr. Jeffress." But it's clear where I rank! Now, don't misunderstand me; I couldn't care less about where I rank on someone's list of personal preferences. But it's all too easy for Christians to start believing that the messenger is more important than the message. Paul wrote to the Christians in Corinth, "I have been informed concerning you . . . that there are quarrels among you. Now I mean this, that each one of you is saying, 'I am of Paul,' and 'I of Apollos,' and 'I of Cephas [Peter]'" (1 Cor. 1:11–12). But he was having none of it. He explained that Paul, Apollos, and Peter were servants of Christ. Each man may have had a unique ministry, "but God . . . causes the growth" of His church (3:7). It's a nice way of saying, "Quit comparing one preacher to another preacher. Quit pretending that the preacher is more important than the one whom the preacher is supposed to be preaching about."

But there is one more way in which hypocrisy is seen in the church. Whenever we believe lies and disbelieve truth, our spiritual growth becomes stunted. You may have been told as a child that if you didn't eat your vegetables, you'd stunt your growth. That's what hypocrisy does in the church.

Now, it's important to understand that a hypocrite in the church may or may not be a genuine Christian. Some unbelievers pretend to be followers of Christ when they are not. They successfully fool others (and perhaps themselves) into thinking that one day they will be welcomed into heaven. For these hypocrites, they are unable to grow spiritually because they are not saved.

However, there are some genuine Christians who pretend to be more spiritual than they really are. They pretend to have a robust prayer life, they feign love for other people, and they claim to be generous in their giving—but their actions tell another story. These hypocritical Christians become stunted in their spiritual growth because they refuse to exercise truths they believe to be true. And lack of spiritual exercise is one major characteristic of what Paul called "infants in Christ."

When he first came to Corinth preaching the gospel, Paul said, "I . . . could not speak to you as to spiritual men, but as to men of flesh, as to infants in Christ. I gave you milk to drink, not solid food; for you were not yet able to receive it" (1 Cor. 3:1–2). The problem was, by the time Paul wrote the letter we know as 1 Corinthians, four or five years had transpired from when he established the church.[2] It made sense that when Paul first came to the city, he offered the people spiritual milk (the basics of Christianity), since they were not yet ready for spiritual meat (deeper theological truths). However, after so many years, the congregation was no more mature spiritually than when he first arrived. Paul said, "Indeed, even now you are not yet able [to receive spiritual meat], for you are still fleshly" (vv. 2–3).

The writer of Hebrews picked up on Paul's metaphor of milk and solid food in admonishing another group of believers: "Though by this time you ought to be teachers, you have need again for someone to teach you the elementary principles of the oracles of God, and you have come to need milk and not solid food. For everyone who partakes only of milk is not accustomed to the word of righteousness, for he is an infant. But solid food is for the mature, who because of practice have their senses trained to discern good and evil" (Heb. 5:12–14).

Perhaps one of the greatest dangers of hypocrisy within the walls of the church is the destruction it causes outside the church. When unbelievers watch Christian hypocrites, they don't see the attractiveness of the truth; instead, they are repelled by a lie gussied up in religious garb. Christian writer Brennan Manning said, "The greatest single cause of atheism today is Christians who acknowledge Jesus with their lips, then walk out the door and deny Him by their lifestyle."[3] Unbelievers see no reason to believe in God when Christians don't live what we really believe.

The Rewards of Hypocrisy

Like a warning sign painted in big, bold letters, Jesus said,

> Beware of practicing your righteousness before men to be noticed by them; otherwise you have no reward with your Father who is in heaven. (Matt. 6:1)

Notice that if you fail to heed His warning, then you'll not only veer off the true path and potentially lead others into a minefield but also receive no reward from God. Hypocrites trade the eternal applause of God for the temporal applause of people, because when it comes to righteousness and rewards, the formula is either/or, not both/and. You can't have it both ways. You have to make a choice—either God or others.

You might be saying, "Wait a minute, Pastor! Earlier Jesus said, 'Let your light shine *before men* in such a way that they may see your good works' (5:16). So how can He now say, 'Beware of practicing your righteousness *before men* to be noticed by them'? Which is it?"

Pastor John R. W. Stott offered a good answer to this: "Jesus is speaking against different sins. It is our human cowardice which made him say 'let your light shine before others,' and our human vanity which made him tell us to beware of practicing our righteousness in front of others. . . . Our good deeds must be public so that our light shines; our religious devotions must be secret in case we boast about them. Besides, the end of both instructions of Jesus is the same, namely the glory of God."[4]

If our intent is to glorify God, then God will reward us. But if our intent is to glorify ourselves, then we are being hypocritical and God will not reward us.

This raises the question, When are we most tempted to flaunt pretend piety? Essentially, there are three areas Jesus identified for us: when we give (Matt. 6:2), when we pray (v. 5), and when we fast (v. 16).

Each area is an outward expression of our faith—our righteousness put into practice. In fact, the Jews used the same Hebrew word (*tzedakah*) for both "righteousness" and "giving alms," indicating that they believed giving to the poor was automatically considered righteous. One early Jewish saying went, "It is better to give alms than to lay up gold. For almsgiving saves from death, and purges away every sin."[5]

The external acts of giving, praying, and fasting can be paraded, exaggerated, and even faked. But God isn't fooled; He sees the heart. As 1 Samuel 16:7 says, "God sees not as man sees, for man looks at the outward appearance, but the LORD looks at the heart." And Hebrews 4:13 says, "There is no creature hidden from His sight, but all things are open and laid bare to the eyes of Him with whom we have to do."

God sees your every move and motive, so as you put your faith into practice, be sure to do so for the glory of God alone. Don't strut your spirituality or put your piety on parade—and if you do, don't expect a reward from God.

Don't Toot Your Own Horn

The first area in which Jesus said we're tempted to become hypocritical is in our giving to the poor. In biblical days, they called such giving "alms." Since First Baptist Dallas is a downtown church, we have our share of homeless persons who pass by or walk through our campus. It's not unusual to see them on Sunday mornings, holding out their hands and asking for money from people going in or out of the church. Sometimes I give to those asking. Although I know that receiving a few bucks is not a long-term solution to the person's economic woes, it might help them make it through the day.

The poor have always been a part of every society, just as they were in Jesus's day. Of course, almsgiving need not be restricted to giving money; it can also include offering a place to stay, paying for a meal, buying a tank of gas for the stranded, providing clothing and personal hygiene products, giving a job to someone even if only for a day, and just about any other thing you can think of that might help the poor.

Material support is a good thing to provide, and Scripture is filled with commands to help the poor.[6] But there's a right way and a wrong way to help. Jesus first dealt with the wrong way—how we are *not* to give to the poor. He said,

> So when you give to the poor, do not sound a trumpet before you, as the hypocrites do in the synagogues and in the streets, so that they may be honored by men. Truly I say to you, they have their reward in full. (Matt. 6:2)

In ancient Israel, a trumpet (*hazora*) was made from either silver or bronze and consisted of a straight tube, without valves, that flared at the end to create a bell.[7]

Jesus probably had two things in mind when He talked about blowing a trumpet. First, He meant this literally. At the time, priests blew trumpets in the temple when funds were collected for special needs.[8] And since He mentioned blowing a trumpet "in the synagogues and in the streets" (v. 2), Jesus was most likely also referring to the sounding of a trumpet to announce fasts, which included almsgiving. According to scholar G. Campbell Morgan, "Some Pharisees, intending to distribute gifts, would come to a conspicuous place in the city, and blow a small silver trumpet, at which there would gather round him the maimed, the halt [the lame], the blind. Then, with great show of generosity, he would scatter gifts upon them."[9]

Second, Jesus meant "do not sound a trumpet" figuratively (v. 2). In other words, don't toot your own horn. Don't wave the check you wrote to some ministry under other people's noses. Don't announce how much you gave to your church's benevolence fund. Don't brag about all the times you volunteered at the homeless shelter or the houses you helped build with Habitat for Humanity. Don't flaunt your philanthropy by posting pictures of you helping the needy—or the selfie you took with a needy person. Don't tie your generous donation to having your name carved in granite on the building.

Even in this age of online giving, some churches still pass an offering plate on Sunday mornings. I know of people who've written checks and placed them in the offering plate faceup, instead of facedown or folded. I've even heard of people who've thumped the bottom of the plate to draw attention as they placed their money into it. Don't do that. That's tooting your own horn.

In either case, whether blowing a literal trumpet or a figurative one, Jesus said such trumpet players give of their resources not to honor God but "so they may be honored by men" (v. 2)—in order to receive praise from those around them. In the convicting words of Charles Spurgeon, "To stand with a penny in one hand and a trumpet in the other is the posture of hypocrisy,"[10] making us no better than the

Pharisees, whom John said "loved the approval of men rather than the approval of God" (John 12:43).

Whenever we seek the praise of others, we forfeit the praise of God. That's why Jesus said, "Truly I say to you, they have their reward in full" (Matt. 6:2). The phrase "have . . . reward in full" in Greek is *apecho*. It's an economic word, used during commercial transactions when a receipt was given for payment. It literally means "payment in full."

For example, when we had our home painted, the painter handed me a bill after he completed the job. I then paid him, and he gave me a receipt that was stamped with large, red letters: *Paid in Full*. Those three words told both of us that I didn't owe him anything else, and he shouldn't expect anything else. He completed the work, and I paid him. Period. That ended our business dealing—unless I hire him again.

In the same way, Jesus said if you give charitable gifts to impress others with your generosity, then you might get the admiration of those standing nearby or those who read your social media post or your name on the building, but that's all you're going to get—the temporal rewards of today, not the eternal rewards of tomorrow.

Do Practice Discreet Giving

In 2 Corinthians 9:7, the apostle Paul wrote, "God loves a cheerful giver." He also loves an anonymous and secret giver. That's what Jesus said in Matthew 6:3–4: "But when you give to the poor, do not let your left hand know what your right hand is doing, so that your giving will be in secret." The idea comes from magicians' "sleight of hand" when they make a coin disappear. Attention is drawn away from the activity. In the same way, when you give to the Lord's work, everyone's attention ought to be on God while you secretly place your money in the offering plate or make your online donation.

Earlier, Jesus warned us about the hypocrisy of those who blow a trumpet when they give, and He told us not to give that way (v. 2). The only foolproof way to avoid hypocrisy is to give without fanfare. Today, most Christians keep records of our giving to charitable organizations, including churches and ministries like Pathway to Victory. And the organization sends us a receipt of our donations for tax purposes. There's nothing wrong with that. But if we're keeping records so we can brag about how generous we are, that's hypocrisy.

When it comes to giving, hypocrisy usually takes one of three forms. First of all, we can give a false impression, such as pretending to give money to help the needy when we really haven't. Politicians often get caught in this type of hypocrisy. Many give the impression they are extremely generous in providing financial assistance to charitable organizations only to have their hypocrisy exposed when their tax returns are made public.

Second, we can deceive ourselves into believing things about ourselves that aren't true. We can fool ourselves into thinking we're generous givers while giving only 1 to 2 percent of our income, for example. This is called believing your own press releases.

Third, we can deceive others into thinking that our motives are pure when they aren't. I think of the first-century couple Ananias and Sapphira, who wanted to receive the same praise from Christians for their generosity that a man named Barnabas had received without the same degree of sacrifice. In Acts 4:36–5:11, we read that Barnabas gave all the proceeds from a land sale, while Ananias and Sapphira only pretended to give all the money from their sale. Barnabas's motive in giving was to meet the material needs of others, while this couple's motive was to receive the adulation of others. Ananias and Sapphira were the kind of hypocrites Jesus had in mind in this passage. As commentators W. D. Davies and D. C. Allison put it, "They were not giving but *buying*. They wanted the praise of men, they paid for it."[11]

If you want the praise of God, don't flaunt your giving. Pay little attention to your good deeds so God can pay great attention to them. That's the point Jesus was making when He said,

> But when you give to the poor, do not let your left hand know what your right hand is doing, so that your giving will be in secret; and your Father who sees what is done in secret will reward you. (Matt. 6:3–4)

Let's be careful not to let our altruism turn into egotism.

How are we rewarded for our genuine, humble giving? The prosperity preachers on television say we'll be rewarded in some tangible way if we give to their ministries. That may or may not happen, depending on the motive of the giver and the sovereignty of God. But financial reward should never be our motive in giving. The rewards Jesus spoke of don't mean you'll suddenly discover a luxury car in your garage or a lot of money deposited in your bank account. Rather, we should think of it like this: secret giving brings secret rewards.

C. S. Lewis provided helpful insight about this. He wrote, "Money is not the natural reward of love; that is why we call a man mercenary if he marries a woman for the sake of her money. But marriage is the proper reward for a real lover, and he is not mercenary for desiring it. . . . The proper rewards are not simply tacked on to the activity for which they are given, but are the activity itself in consummation."[12]

One of God's most valuable rewards is inner joy, the knowledge that a need has been meet—the hungry are fed, the sick are healed, the homeless are sheltered, the forgotten are remembered, the wayward are restored, and most importantly, the lost are saved. Such generous, quiet giving is a demonstration of divine love in action and brings with it its own spiritual rewards, just as Jesus said: "It is more blessed to give than to receive" (Acts 20:35).

Another one of God's rewards is a clear conscience—knowing that the good from your generosity went to help people and honor God. A friend once said, "Happiness is a life lived under the sunny skies of a clear conscience." Only the generous soul who practices righteousness in private by giving as an act of worship enjoys such rewards.

A Personal Story about Giving

After reading this chapter about giving, you may be wondering, *Pastor, you've talked to us a lot about money, but what about your own story? Has there been any event in your life that shaped your attitude about money and about giving it to God's work?* Yes. There are several stories I could share with you, but one in particular stands out because it was my first time giving sacrificially and seeing God's faithfulness.

When I was in high school, my very first job was working for a Christian bookstore. I made the minimum wage at the time, $2.10 an hour. I worked every shift I could, and finally I accumulated $700. And I felt like I was John D. Rockefeller! I was really proud of having $700 in my checking account.

At the same time, I was also volunteering with a little church in McKinney, Texas. One night during the evening worship service, the pastor stood up and said, "God has given me a vision to start a bus ministry for our church. There are hundreds of boys and girls around here we could bus in to hear the gospel and be saved. The only problem is, we don't have any buses, and we don't have any money to purchase the buses. So let's pray about it, church, and see if we can collect an offering to buy the buses." Well, God spoke to me right then. I didn't like what I heard at first. He told me to write a check for the entire $700 to donate to the bus ministry. I have to admit, I struggled a little bit with that. I thought about all the floors I had mopped, all the commodes I had cleaned, everything I had done to earn that money. I thought, *Is this really God speaking to me?* But I made a decision that night. I remember deciding I didn't want to get into the habit of ignoring God's voice. So I prayed, "God, if You've said it, then I'm going to do it." So I happily wrote a check for $700. The church got the buses. Over the next couple of years, we saw many boys and girls come to faith in Christ.

But the interesting side note to this experience came after I'd written that check. Now, I'm not saying this happens all the time; it's my story. Suddenly, God provided all these extra jobs for me to do. Back then I played the accordion for money, and I began to get job offers for weddings, bar mitzvahs, and funeral receptions, where I could make in one night of playing my accordion a week's worth of wages from the bookstore.

Within just a couple of months, my bank account was back up and exceeded that $700.

I learned two lessons from that experience that I've never forgotten. One is you can't outgive God. You just can't. We used to have a member of our church who was a great Christian businesswoman. She wore a necklace that had two shovels on it: a little shovel and a big shovel. People used to ask her, "What does that mean?" And she would say, "This little shovel is what I give to God; I shovel it up to heaven. The big shovel is God's shovel; it's what He gives to me in return." And then she would smile and say, "God's got a bigger shovel than I do." You can't outgive God.

The second thing I learned from those experiences is that if you're a Christian, there is no greater joy than using your time and investing your resources in making sure people are going to be in heaven. A. W. Tozer once said, "Whatever is given to Christ is immediately touched with immortality."[13] Isn't that an interesting thought? What we do with our money during our brief time on earth, as insignificant as it may seem, matters forever.

If you will listen for the voice of God in your giving, He will speak to you. And if you obey, He will provide for you and bless you—not always with money but always with the reward of knowing that you've made a difference for eternity. That's why Jesus said, "Your Father who sees what is done in secret will reward you" (Matt. 6:4). Today, maybe your prayer could be, "God, show me what You would have me to do. Show me what I can give to make the best investment I can make in Your kingdom today."

seven

Straight Talk about
Your Prayer Life

WHAT'S THE MOST REVOLUTIONARY IDEA in human history? Would you say it was Copernicus's discovery that the earth orbits the sun and not the other way around? How about Isaac Newton's insights into gravity when the apple fell on his head? What about the invention of movable type with Johannes Gutenberg's printing press, or Thomas Edison's incandescent light bulb? Perhaps it's something more modern, like the invention of the personal computer or the internet or the smartphone.

Would you be surprised if I told you none of those ideas or inventions are the most amazing, earth-shattering reality in human history? That distinction is as old as humanity—and it was God's idea: we can talk with the Creator of the universe.

Right about now you might be yawning, thinking something like, *Come on, Pastor! There's nothing duller and more unrevolutionary than prayer. Just come to my church some Sunday and listen to my pastor pray.*

Before you skip this chapter, hear me out for just a moment. It's true that the way prayer is often taught and practiced in our churches today is about as exciting as eating a mashed potato sandwich. But that's not how Jesus taught about prayer. Pastor and author Max Lucado got it right when he wrote, "Prayer . . . impact[s] the flow of history. God has wired his world for power, but he calls on us to flip the switch."[1]

I don't know whether Lucado was reading theologian Karl Barth when he wrote those words, but he could have been. Barth also understood something about prayer: if we followed Jesus's way, prayer would be revolutionary. Historians say the purpose of a revolution is to shake up the world order. That's just what Barth said: "To clasp the hands in prayer is the beginning of an uprising against the disorder of the world."[2] What could be more revolutionary than that?

Of course, this raises the question, Are we praying the way Jesus taught? Perhaps you grew up in a Christian home. If so, praying was likely part of your upbringing. But there's a danger in that. You may be like folks who live in Colorado, where snowcapped mountains are commonplace and no longer take their breath away. But flatlanders and city dwellers like me travel hundreds or even thousands of miles to spend a few days in the mountains to take in the beauty. I guarantee you, for those few days we really experience the mountains!

In the same way, those who have become numb to the beauty and power of prayer need to see prayer in a new way.

When Jesus taught about prayer in the Sermon on the Mount, He gave His followers a pattern we often call the Lord's Prayer. In this chapter, we'll take a close look at the Lord's Prayer to help us see it anew—and realize that prayer really is revolutionary.

How *Not* to Pray

At the beginning of Matthew 6, Jesus gave this warning: "Beware of practicing your righteousness before men to be noticed by them" (v. 1). If we fail to heed Jesus's warning, He added, then "you have no reward with your Father who is in heaven" (v. 1), meaning that we will forfeit God's eternal praise. Jesus called such religious displays dishonest and hypocritical, and He applied His warning against hypocrisy to three key areas in which we practice our faith: giving, praying, and fasting.

In verses 2–4, Jesus talked about hypocritical giving. In verses 16–18, He talked about hypocritical fasting—the kind that walks around making a public show of it, hoping others will point to us and say, "There goes a godly person."[3] Between these two, in verses 5–15, Jesus addressed the issue of prayer, teaching us first how *not* to pray.

Don't Brag When You Pray

As He did when introducing the subject of giving, Jesus introduced the subject of prayer by giving an example of what *not* to do. He said,

> When you pray, you are not to be like the hypocrites; for they love to stand and pray in the synagogues and on the street

corners so that they may be seen by men. Truly I say to you, they have their reward in full. (Matt. 6:5)

Was Jesus condemning public prayer? Not at all. Some of the most powerful prayers in the Bible were prayed publicly, such as Elijah's prayer on Mount Carmel that resulted in the fire of God falling from heaven to consume the burnt sacrifice (1 Kings 18:36–38). And Jesus's miracle of feeding thousands with a young boy's sack lunch was preceded by a very public prayer (Matt. 14:19).

When Jesus cautioned His listeners about the dangers of public praying, He was referring to a common abuse by the religious leaders of His day. Whether on street corners or in synagogues, the scribes and Pharisees loved to pray with their hands stretched out, palms facing upward, sometimes with their heads bowed low and sometimes with their heads held high. Many people in our congregations today do the same thing, especially during times of worship as a sincere expression of their devotion to and dependence upon God. But the scribes and Pharisees practiced these physical postures to be admired by others. The bottom-line problem with the Pharisees' intercession was not their *mode* of praying but rather their *motive*.

You see, Jesus isn't concerned about the place or the posture of your prayer, but He is concerned about the purpose of your prayer. Bible commentator William Barclay wrote, "When a man thinks more of *how* he is praying than of *what* he is praying, his prayer dies upon his lips."[4]

A good illustration of this is in Luke 18. In this parable, a Pharisee stood with his face toward heaven and "was praying this to himself: 'God, I thank You that I am not like other people: swindlers, unjust, adulterers, or even like this tax collector. I fast twice a week; I pay tithes of all that I get'" (vv. 11–12). But the tax collector stood alone with his head bowed, beating his breast and saying, "God, be merciful to me, the sinner!" (v. 13). Jesus said, "I tell you, this man went to his house justified rather than the other [the Pharisee]; for everyone who exalts himself will be humbled, but he who humbles himself will be exalted" (v. 14). To God, motive is what matters most.

What does this mean for us? If you're called upon to pray in public, whether over a family meal or with your friend at lunch or before your Sunday school class, and you're more concerned about how your prayer sounds to others than you are about whether it glorifies God, then it's best to decline the offer. You'd be better off going into the privacy of your home and speaking privately with the Father, because Jesus was serious when He said, "Beware of practicing your righteousness before men to be noticed by them" (Matt. 6:1).

Now, God doesn't judge us if we choose not to pray in public. But He does judge us if we offer a public prayer that is focused on impressing others. In Luke 19:22, Jesus said, "By your own words I will judge you." Since that's true, we ought to examine our motives before opening our mouths to pray in public, because to pray only to impress others is to invite the judgment of God. We'd be better off keeping our mouths shut.

Don't Babble When You Pray

In Matthew 6:5, Jesus warned about strutting our spiritual stuff in public prayer, like the scribes and Pharisees, then

He warned against babbling in our prayers, like the Gentile pagans. He said,

> And when you are praying, do not use meaningless repetition as the Gentiles do, for they suppose that they will be heard for their many words. So do not be like them; for your Father knows what you need before you ask Him. (vv. 7–8)

The Greek word translated as "meaningless repetition" in this verse is *battalogeo*. It's an unusual word, and Matthew used it as an onomatopoeia, where the sound of the word reveals its meaning—in this case, "babble" or "babbling." In fact, some translations use the phrase "do not keep on babbling" (NIV) or "don't babble on and on" (NLT).

Pagan prayers in Jesus's day often relied on lengthy ramblings and repetition. Since Jesus was speaking to His followers, He didn't need to warn them against praying to idols. But He did warn them about mimicking the practices of pagans, who believed they could persuade their gods to listen if they said the right words in the right order and then hit the repeat button. As commentator Richard C. H. Lenski wrote, "It is heathen folly to measure prayer by the yard."[5] Don't do that. Don't pray with all words and no meaning. Don't speak without thinking, mindlessly murmuring sounds in long-winded, babbling prayers.

When it comes to prayer, follow Solomon's advice: "Do not be quick with your mouth, do not be hasty in your heart to utter anything before God. God is in heaven and you are on earth, so let your words be few" (Eccles. 5:2 NIV). John Calvin agreed. Commenting on Jesus's warning in Matthew 6:7–8, Calvin wrote, "The grace of God is not obtained by an unmeaning flow of words; but, on the contrary, a devout heart throws out its affections, like an arrow, to pierce heaven."[6]

I still laugh about a prayer meeting my parents once attended and later told me about. A particularly pious individual decided to try to impress the congregants (and God, I presume) with his intercessory skills, using lofty words and theological vocabulary. (I can just picture God in heaven looking at His watch, wondering, *When is this windbag going to be finished?*) Finally, the man approached the grand finale of his prayer with a particularly eloquent conclusion: "And, Lord, when the time comes for us to part this earth and we cross over the . . ." He struggled to remember the word *Jordan*, so he backed up and tried again, "And when the time comes for us to part this earth and we cross over the . . . *equator!*" With that, the congregation burst into laughter, and the man's air of pseudo-piety was punctured.

When we pray, whether in public or in private, our words ought to be like arrows piercing heaven, not like foam darts shot from a child's toy, barely reaching the ceiling. To do that, we need to sharpen our words. Meaningless, thoughtless words and phrases (like "bless" and "cross over the Jordan") dull our prayers and usually lead to rambling repetition. So when you are speaking with God, think carefully about what you want to say. If it helps, write out your prayers. And don't worry if that seems contrived. Remember, God judges our motives.

Keep in mind, God loves you and is more ready to answer your prayers than you are ready to pray. You don't have to extract His gifts as if you're a beggar trying to talk a tightwad out of a few bucks. Your heavenly Father doesn't need to be pestered, battered, or flattered to answer your prayers. Just tell God what's on your heart. Jesus said He already "knows what you need before you ask Him" (Matt. 6:8). He isn't ignorant and doesn't need our instruction. He isn't hesitant and doesn't need our persuasion. But He wants us to ask.

Also, don't come to God in prayer and then let your mind wander. I've always appreciated these words from Max Lucado: "Most of us struggle with prayer. We forget to pray, and when we remember, we hurry through prayers with hollow words. Our minds drift; our thoughts scatter like a covey of quail. Why is this? Prayer requires minimal effort. No location is prescribed. No particular clothing is required. No title or office is stipulated. Yet you'd think we were wrestling a greased pig."[7]

But why? Prayer is simply speaking to God, who wants to bless us. All He asks is that our motives are right and that we concentrate and speak clearly, praying as if we were speaking with our spouse or a close friend about something important. That's not too much to ask.

How to Pray

In contrast to the Jewish hypocrites who prayed in public to be praised for their piety, and the Gentile pagans who prayed to their gods using meaningless words that sounded like babbling, Jesus gave His followers two alternatives for how to pray.

Pray in Secret

In Matthew 6:6, Jesus said,

> But you, when you pray, go into your inner room, close your door and pray to your Father who is in secret, and your Father who sees what is done in secret will reward you.

Again, the point Jesus was making isn't so much between public prayer and private prayer. Anyone, whether in public or private, can become a braggart (a hypocrite) or a babbler (a pagan). Remember, as we saw in Jesus's parable, the Pharisee and the tax collector were both praying in a public place, the temple—but the Pharisee "was praying . . . *to himself*" (Luke 18:11).

There's no doubt the Pharisee in Jesus's story wasn't interested in glorifying God. Neither hypocrites nor pagans are thinking about God when they pray. Hypocrites think about their own glory, and pagans think about things other than God. Hypocrites misuse the *purpose* of prayer by degrading it from the glory of God to the glory of self. Pagans misuse the *nature* of prayer by degrading it from personal communication with God to mere repetition of words.

Jesus calls us to something better, something higher—something revolutionary: authentic, intelligent, and God-focused prayer, both in private and in public.

The great thing about private prayer is that there's no one to impress. We certainly won't impress God, who knows what's on our hearts even before we've figured out how to put it into words. So when we go into our rooms to speak with our heavenly Father, intending to glorify Him, He's happy to reward us. In fact, according to scholar R. V. G. Tasker, the Greek word Jesus used for "inner room" (*tameion*) "was used for the store-room where treasures might be kept." The implication is that "there are treasures already awaiting" us when we pray with the right motives and proper attention, which more times than not happens when we pray in secret.[8]

Do you have a place where you can be alone with God? Throughout my life I've had special places where I would go to pray. When I was in high school, it was in a park across from the school I attended; when I was first married, it was a baseball field several blocks from our home; and now, it is by the couch in my office. But regardless of the location, I've tried to set appointments with God when I can meet with Him privately and tell Him what is on my heart.

Are you taking time in your day for private conversations with the Lord? Maybe a good time for you to spend in prayer is when you're in the car, driving to work or running errands. Turn off the radio and spend those minutes praising God for who He is and what He's done in your life, asking Him to glorify Himself by revealing His will to you and giving you the desire and strength to accomplish it. And then ask Him to meet your daily needs, to forgive your sins and give you grace to forgive others, and to protect you from temptation. (But keep your hands on the steering wheel and your eyes on the road!) These conversations with God will transform not only your drive time but your life.

In seminary, I made a life-changing discovery about the connection between private and public prayer. It was this: *my effectiveness in prayer in public is directly correlated to my effectiveness in prayer in private*. I learned this lesson by listening carefully to the public prayers of one of my professors. Whenever he prayed before class, I felt as if I were transported to the very throne room of God. The presence of our professor, his vocal tones, and the words he spoke were lost in the wonder of the sense that God was in the center of everything he said. My professor didn't pray to impress the class; he prayed to glorify God and to help us worship God before class began. I realized that my professor could only pray like that in public because he prayed like that in private.

True godliness, which is one of God's great rewards, comes only after spending time alone with God—praying in secret.

Pray Simply

Whether we are praying in public or in private, our prayers ought to be simple (avoiding words like *Jordan* and *equator*!). There's no need for long, complex prayers made up of complicated theological words that require a dictionary to understand. Simple and straightforward is just fine—and that is just how Jesus taught His disciples to pray in Matthew 6:9–15.[9]

There's nothing wrong with praying the Lord's Prayer word for word, but Jesus's purpose was to provide His followers with a model for effective prayer, not a mantra to be repeated verbatim. He said, "Pray, then, *in this way*," not, "Pray this specific prayer." As such, this prayer can be personalized for each individual situation.

Although this prayer in Matthew 6, as well as the version found in Luke 11, is often called the Lord's Prayer, it really should be called the Disciples' Prayer, since it's not really a prayer Jesus prayed—or could pray completely. Jesus, the sinless Son of God, never needed to seek forgiveness of sins, which makes up the last half of the prayer. It's only the Lord's Prayer in the sense that Jesus taught us to pray "in this way":

> Our Father who is in heaven,
> Hallowed be Your name.
> Your kingdom come.
> Your will be done,
> On earth as it is in heaven.
> Give us this day our daily bread.

> And forgive us our debts, as we also have forgiven
>   our debtors.
> And do not lead us into temptation, but deliver
>   us from evil. [For Yours is the kingdom and
>   the power and the glory forever. Amen.] (Matt.
>   6:9–13)

Jesus began, "Our Father who is in heaven" (v. 9). The word *father* in English is a formal term. It's probably true in your home as it is in mine—when my daughters are talking to me, they usually don't address me as "Father" but call me "Dad." Similarly, when Jesus instructed us to pray, "Our Father," He didn't use a formal term. Everyday life at the time of Jesus was carried out in the Aramaic language, a close cousin to Hebrew. The Aramaic word Jesus used here was *Abba*. It's what Jesus would likely have called Joseph, His earthly father. It meant something like "Daddy," but with more reverence, more like "Dearest Daddy." To Jesus, the intimacy of prayer brought with it an intimacy of address.

God is the Father of all who place their faith in Christ. That's captured in the word *our*. He is *our* Father, not just *mine* or *yours*. This means we are brothers and sisters in Christ; we are part of the same divine family.

But even though God is our Dearest Daddy, whose love is good and great, we must never forget that He is "in heaven." God is transcendent and sovereign over His creation, wielding power and authority as "the only wise God" (Rom. 16:27). Whatever His fatherly love directs, His kingly power is able to perform.

By directing us to approach God as "Our Father who is in heaven," Jesus wasn't establishing appropriate etiquette, as if we were addressing the queen of England with genuflection and "Your Majesty." Rather, Jesus was encouraging us to remember that God is our loving, powerful Father, which puts us in the right frame of mind before asking Him to do something on our behalf. It's always wise, before launching into your petitions in prayer, to spend time thinking about who God is. Then, when you present your requests to Him, you ask with humility, confidence, and awe. You are concerned more about God's name, kingdom, and will than having your needs met.

The Particulars of Prayer

Next, let's look at the particulars of the prayer. There are six petitions in the Lord's Prayer, each connected to God's coming kingdom. The first three concern God; the second three concern us. This order is intentional. God's concerns should always come before ours, because His interests are more important than ours.

First, *pray for God's reputation to be honored in your life*. Jesus put it like this: "Hallowed be Your name" (Matt. 6:9). The Greek word translated as "hallowed" is *hagiazo*. It means "to treat something or someone as holy, to give reverence to." Of course, God is already holy, so Jesus wasn't saying we ought to pray that God would become holy or more holy. I think Jesus had two things in mind here. Number one, when we hallow God's name, we treat it as special in our prayers. We affirm what is already true about God—that His attributes, His character, and His activities are all good, loving, and right. And number two, when we hallow God's name, we ought to pray that others come to acknowledge God's holiness as well. One way to do this is to place others ahead of ourselves, as Jesus did. In Philippians 2:3–4, the apostle Paul said, "Do nothing from selfishness or empty conceit, but with humility of mind regard one another as more important than yourselves; do not merely look out for your own personal interests, but also for the interests of others."

Second, *pray for God's justice and mercy to reign in your life*. Jesus said, "Your kingdom come" (Matt. 6:10). I love the way *The Message* translates this: "Set the world right." This petition won't be fully accomplished until Christ returns to earth and sets up His earthly kingdom during the millennium. The book of Revelation describes the millennium as the thousand-year reign of Christ on earth that follows immediately on the heels of the seven years of tribulation, which follows the rapture of the church, which could occur at any moment. The millennial kingdom obviously hasn't come yet, or Jesus wouldn't instruct us to pray for its coming. But it is imminent, so we need to be prepared for that day.

So I have to ask: Are you ready for when that day comes? The primary way to get ready for the coming kingdom is to trust in Jesus Christ as your Savior. Once you've done that—or if you've already done that—then ask the Lord to prepare you for His coming. Then you can pray as John did when he recorded the last prayer in the Bible: "Amen. Come, Lord Jesus" (Rev. 22:20). But until that day when Jesus returns and sets up His kingdom, we can ask God to bring about kingdom-like activities on earth—to right wrongs and to turn things that are upside down right side up.

Third, *pray for God's will to be done in your life*. Jesus taught us to pray, "Your will be done, on earth as it is in heaven" (Matt. 6:10). Of course, this will happen fully and perfectly when Jesus Christ reigns on earth in His kingdom, but we ought to ask the Lord for His will to be accomplished in the intervening years. According to Romans 12:2, the will of God is "good and acceptable and perfect." It's foolish for us to resist God's will but wise for us to desire, discern, and do it.

Pastor Kent Hughes made this prayer request personal when he wrote, "When we pray this prayer, we are asking God to do what is necessary to make his will prevail in our lives. And God then comes with gracious, kind violence to root out all impediments to our obedience. To pray this prayer may terrify us, but it will also deliver us from ourselves."[10]

What does God need to uproot in your life? Whatever it is, don't resist. Rather, invite Him to come with His hoe and spade and get to work.

Having prayed for God's glory, we are now ready to pray for God's grace. The last three petitions of the Lord's Prayer focus on three essential needs: sustenance for today, forgiveness for yesterday, and protection for tomorrow.

Fourth, *pray for God to take care of your daily needs.* Jesus said, "Give us this day our daily bread" (Matt. 6:11). "Bread" is a stand-in for all our physical needs—healthy food, clean water, safe shelter, and anything else necessary for the preservation of life. "Daily" reflects first-century life, in which workers received their pay daily and could usually only buy what they needed for that day's meals. So Jesus was telling us to ask God to meet whatever *needs* (not greeds) we have today.

His point was this: we are dependent upon God to meet our needs day in, day out. Every heartbeat and every breath happen because God is meeting our daily needs. I know we like to think of ourselves as independent, with the ability to pull ourselves up by our own bootstraps. But have you ever tried to pull yourself up by your bootstraps? It's impossible. So every day we look to God and ask Him to pull us up.

Asking God to meet our daily needs doesn't release us from our responsibility to work, though. Paul said, "If anyone is not willing to work, then he is not to eat, either" (2 Thess. 3:10). In fact, one of the ways God answers this petition is by giving us the ability and opportunity to earn a living. In Deuteronomy 8:18, Moses wrote, "You shall remember the LORD your God, for it is He who is giving you power to make wealth." So get to work, and "do your work heartily, as for the Lord rather than for men, knowing that from the Lord you will receive the reward of the inheritance. It is the Lord Christ whom you serve" (Col. 3:23–24).

Asking God to meet our daily needs also doesn't mean we're free to ignore those around us who need help. After all, the prayer is "Give *us* this day *our* daily bread," not "Give *me* this day *my* daily bread." God may very well choose to answer this prayer in someone else's life through you.

Fifth, *pray for God to forgive you and make you a forgiver.* Jesus couldn't have been any clearer when He said, "And forgive us our debts, as we also have forgiven our debtors" (Matt. 6:12). The most common Greek word for sin is *hamartia*, meaning "to miss the mark or target." But that's not the word Jesus used here. In this prayer, He used *opheilemata*, the Greek word for debt. It refers to a failure to pay fully what is owed. What Jesus had in mind is the debt we owe to God for falling short of the perfection He requires (5:48). We could never pay this debt in our own righteousness, so we humble ourselves and ask for forgiveness.

Jesus expanded this idea of forgiveness and applied it in the second half of Matthew 6:12 and in verses 14–15:

> And forgive us our debts, as we also have forgiven our debtors. . . .
>
> For if you forgive others for their transgressions, your heavenly Father will also forgive you. But if you do not forgive others, then your Father will not forgive your transgressions.

Don't misunderstand what Jesus was saying. He wasn't hinting at some sort of salvation by works or implying that we can earn God's forgiveness by forgiving others. Forgiving others is a demonstration of just how much we need forgiveness from God. In another context, when a prostitute anointed His feet with perfume, Jesus linked forgiveness with love. He said, "Her sins, which are many, have been forgiven, for she loved much; but he who is forgiven little, loves little" (Luke 7:47).

Who has wronged you and needs your forgiveness? Don't be like the man who, when he found out he had been bitten by a rabid dog, sat down and made a list of all the people he wanted to bite. Rather, make a list of all the people you need to forgive. Remember, Jesus was very clear that if we refuse to forgive others, God will refuse to forgive us. As Thomas Fuller once said, "He that cannot forgive others, breaks the bridge over which he must pass himself, for every man has need to be forgiven."[11]

Sixth, *pray for God to protect you from temptation.* In the next part of His prayer, Jesus said, "And do not lead us into temptation, but deliver us from evil" (Matt. 6:13). Now, that raises an important question: Does God ever tempt us? Doesn't it stand to reason that if Jesus said, "Pray that God wouldn't lead you into temptation," then maybe sometimes God does lead you into temptation? Why would you pray this prayer if it were not a possibility?

Let me be clear: God never tempts His children. James 1:13–14 says, "Let no one say when he is tempted, 'I am being tempted by God'; for God cannot be tempted by evil, and He Himself does not tempt anyone. But each one is tempted when he is carried away and enticed by his own lust."

We can never say, "I am being tempted by God." God does not tempt anyone. He has zero to do with it. You know why temptation comes? James told us: we are tempted whenever we are "carried away," which means drawn by an inward power, and "enticed," which means hooked, by our own lust. James said we fall into sin because we have corrupt desires on the inside and because Satan is dangling the right bait in front of us on the outside.

So how do we reconcile what James said, that God has no part in our temptation, with Jesus's prayer that teaches us to ask God, "Do not lead us into temptation"? The only way to understand this apparent contradiction in Scripture is to know the difference between *temptation* and *testing*.

In English, we have two different words. On one hand is the word *temptation*, which means to entice to do evil. God never entices anybody to do evil. He never creates evil or acts evilly. He never wants people to commit evil. God is never involved in tempting people. That's what Satan does. He tempts people in order to destroy them.

On the other hand, in English, is the word *test*. A test is a difficult circumstance that is used to strengthen our faith.

The Bible says God tests people all the time. He tests His children, not to destroy them but to strengthen them. That's why James also says, "Consider it all joy, my brethren, when you encounter various trials, knowing that the testing of your faith produces endurance" (vv. 2–3).

Here's where it gets interesting. Even though we have these two different words in English, in the Greek language there's only one word, *peirasmós*. That word sometimes means *temptation*, an enticement to do evil. And that same word sometimes means *test*, a difficult situation to strengthen our faith. The meaning of the word depends on its context.

A difficult situation can be both a temptation and a test at the same time. Let's say the doctor says you have cancer. Is that a temptation or a test? Well, Satan will try to use that difficult situation to tempt you to deny God, to destroy your faith. So, for Satan, it's a temptation. But at the same time, God is using that difficult situation to test you, to strengthen your faith. Whether that difficult situation ends up being a temptation that destroys your faith or a test that strengthens your faith depends on your response to it.

Difficult situations are neither good nor bad. They're a temptation or a test depending upon our response to them. So whenever we're praying this prayer, we're saying, "Lord, do not lead us into difficult situations."

Timeless Truths about Tests in Our Lives

I think as Christians we have almost romanticized difficult situations. We think somehow they're these wonderful tests that come into our lives. No, they're really not. Yes, they could strengthen us—but they also could destroy us. And so, like Jesus, we should pray, "Lord, if it's all the same to You, please keep these things from happening to me." But we also know, like Jesus discovered, that sometimes God has a different plan for us. Instead of sparing us from problems, God's plan is to take us through our problems.

That's why Jesus added the second part of this petition: "But deliver us from evil" (Matt. 6:13). That is a prayer for protection through problems. You may be facing the greatest challenge you have ever faced. Maybe it's the breakup of a relationship. Maybe it's a rebellious child. It may be the loss of a job. It may be the loss of a dream. And right now you feel separated from God. Maybe you have prayed over and over again, "Lord, deliver me out of this problem." And up to this point, God has said no. He is telling you, *My plan is to take you through this problem*. If that's true for you, if it appears that God's plan for your life is for you to go through this difficulty, then let me share with you three timeless truths that will help you when you're going through the crucible of testing.

Our Tests Don't Surprise God

First, our tests do not take God by surprise. Whether God directly caused the difficulty you're experiencing, whether He allowed Satan to cause it, or whether your problem is simply the result of your own poor choices—whatever the reason for your suffering—it didn't take God by surprise. In Psalm 139:16, David said that every detail of every day of our lives was written in God's book before we ever took our first breath. Isn't that an amazing thought? Before the foundation of the world, God wrote down every detail of your life and my life. And God not only knew every detail but also planned each one for a great eternal purpose. When you go through that failed marriage, when you go through that bankruptcy, when you go through that loss of an important relationship in your life, when you're going through cancer, God doesn't slap His forehead and say, "Oh, I can't believe that happened. What are we going to do now?" These things are not detours from God's plan for your life; they are a part of God's plan for your life. A plan for your good.

Our Tests Reveal God's Love

Second, the tests that come into our lives are evidence of God's love for us. Here's an interesting fact: search through the Bible and you will never find God testing the ungodly. There's no instance when God ever tested the heathen nations, only Israel. Furthermore, He never tested unbelievers, only believers. Think about Abraham, who was known as the friend of God. Abraham was a man of faith, yet Genesis 22:1 says, "God tested Abraham." Why? Not to destroy Abraham's faith but to strengthen it. Tests are God's vote of confidence in us. They are evidence of His love for us.

Our Tests Are Momentary

Third, our tests are momentary, but God's faithfulness is forever. In his book *A Grace Disguised*, Jerry Sittser described his struggle to make sense out of an automobile accident that took the life of his wife, his daughter, and his mother all at the same time. He wrote, "Loss creates a barren present, as if one were sailing on a vast sea of nothingness. Those who suffer loss live suspended between a past for which they long and a future for which they hope. They want to return to the harbor of the familiar past and recover what was lost. . . . Or they want to sail on and discover a meaningful future that promises to bring them life again. . . . Instead, they find themselves living in a barren present that is empty of meaning."[12]

Perhaps you can identify with those words. You've lost something important to you. You feel like you're on that sea of nothingness. And you have some serious questions about God. You wonder, *God, do You know about my situation? Do You care about my situation? Do You even exist?*

Corrie ten Boom is often credited with saying, "When a train goes through a tunnel and it gets dark, you don't throw away the ticket and jump off. You sit still and trust the engineer." You may be going through that tunnel of testing right now. This is not the time to abandon your faith and jump off. Jesus said this is the time to trust the Engineer to lead you safely to the other side.

After pointing us to God through the six petitions in the Lord's Prayer, Jesus ended this prayer with a doxology that points us back to our trustworthy God:

For Yours is the kingdom and the power and the glory forever. Amen" (Matt. 6:13).[13]

eight

Straight Talk about Your Money

YOU'VE PROBABLY HEARD OF HOWARD HUGHES, the billionaire recluse who shut himself up in his Las Vegas penthouse, watching the same movie over and over and refusing to bathe, cut his hair, or trim his nails. A germophobe, Hughes washed his hands until they became red and raw. But all his money couldn't protect him from germs real and imagined—or buy him the peace of mind he so desperately craved.

However, there's a good chance you've never heard of Elizabeth Johnson Williams. Though she wasn't obsessed with germs, she was like Hughes in many ways. She made a fortune in the cattle business and through savvy real estate investments. When she married, she had to bail her husband out of debt to the tune of $50,000, then she made him sign a prenuptial agreement—and that was in the 1880s.

When her husband died, Lizzie became a recluse, moving into a building she owned in downtown Austin, Texas. One day, a grandnephew visited her. Not seeing anything to eat, he offered to get dinner for her. She refused, insisting that she had plenty to eat. "Where?" he asked. She took a cover from a plate and showed him a piece of cheese and a few crackers. The cover kept the rats from running off with her meal.

Lizzie was so tightfisted that even in the depths of winter she burned only one piece of firewood at a time. At her death in 1924, her net worth was estimated somewhere between $188,000 and $220,000. Adjusted for inflation, her net worth today would be somewhere between $2.8 and $3.3 million.[1]

Yet with all that money, she couldn't enjoy it. She was caught in the grip of loving money more than her needs, believing that fulfillment in life consisted of accumulating more and more wealth. We know this is a lie, but the tug toward materialism is strong, making many of us teeter between what the Bible says and what the advertisements sell, between the eternal riches of Christ and the temporal riches of cash. If we lose our balance, it results in anxiety.

Money and worry are traveling companions. Those who have lots of money worry about losing it; those who have little money worry about getting more of it. Jesus explained that when it comes to wealth and worry, we have a choice to make. In Matthew 6:19–34, He laid out this choice using stark contrasts—we must choose either treasures in heaven or treasures on earth, eyes that see or eyes that don't see, and God as master or money as master. How do we choose, and which is the wise choice?

In this chapter, we'll look first at wealth and then at worry. Then we'll bring them together with some practical suggestions for maintaining a healthy perspective on our money.

A Word about Wealth

I should state for the record that money isn't evil. Having money doesn't make you a sinner, and not having money doesn't make you a saint. Some of the godliest men and women I know are people of means, as were some in the Bible, such as Abraham, David, Solomon, Esther, and Lydia. And I know many godly individuals who are far from being considered rich, as were some in the Bible, such as Caleb, Ruth, John the Baptist, and Peter. Jesus Himself said, "The foxes have holes and the birds of the air have nests, but the Son of Man has nowhere to lay His head" (Matt. 8:20).

Money and possessions alone do not determine a person's spiritual condition. Yes, David said in 1 Chronicles 29:12 that "both riches and honor" come from the Lord, and we ought to praise Him for the material blessings He gives us. But our spiritual condition is determined by whether those material blessings own and possess *us*.

The Bible has a great deal to say about money. For example:

- God is the one who gives us the ability and opportunity to earn money (Deut. 8:18).
- God expects us to provide for ourselves and for our families (2 Thess. 3:10; 1 Tim. 5:8).
- The wise person works hard to save and invest for lean years (Prov. 6:6–11) and to meet the needs of others generously (13:22; 22:9).
- If we've earned our living honestly, then we have every right to enjoy what God provides (1 Tim. 4:3–4; 6:17).

However, if we grow to *love* money, then we've fallen into sin. The apostle Paul said, "The *love* of money is a root of all sorts of evil, and some by longing for it have wandered away from the faith and pierced themselves with many griefs" (1 Tim. 6:10). Whenever we start to love money, we hoard what we have instead of being generous (James 5:2–3). We become materialists, always wanting more. So in Matthew 6:19–24, Jesus warned us against, as scholar Darrell L. Bock put it, "the accumulation of massive amounts of treasure as a life goal."[2]

Two Treasures: Heaven and Earth

Jesus began His talk on worry and wealth with a contrast:

Do not store up for yourselves treasures on earth, where moth and rust destroy, and where thieves break in and steal. But store up for yourselves treasures in heaven, where neither moth nor rust destroys, and where thieves do not break in or steal. (Matt. 6:19–20)

Now, it's pretty clear He was talking about those who love the things of earth more than the things of heaven. But what does it mean to "store up"?

It doesn't mean to make provision for the future—that's wise. Rather, it means to single-mindedly pursue something. In regard to earthly treasure, it means to become greedy—and that is what Jesus warned against. In Luke 12:15, He said, "Be on your guard against every form of greed; for not even when one has an abundance does his life consist of his possessions."

It's foolish, Jesus explained, to invest your time, energy, and resources to chase temporal wealth instead of eternal wealth.

His reasoning was quite simple: material wealth can evaporate like the morning mist. King Solomon, one of the wealthiest men in history, said, "Do not weary yourself to gain wealth, cease from your consideration of it. When you set your eyes on it, it is gone. For wealth certainly makes itself wings like an eagle that flies toward the heavens" (Prov. 23:4–5).

Jesus gave us three reasons wealth disappears. First, He said moths can eat us out of house and home (Matt. 6:19). Jesus was thinking about a rich person's closet. Not much has changed from the first to the twenty-first century, when we still judge the worth of people by what they wear. In Jesus's day, wealthy people wore purple-dyed tunics or robes, sort of like wearing Prada, Gucci, or Yves Saint Laurent today. The dye was made from sea snails harvested off the coast of Tyre (present-day Lebanon), which when boiled secreted a chemical that turned purple when it came into contact with oxygen. A thousand snails were needed to produce one ounce of what was known as Tyrian purple dye.[3] But whether it's a finely woven purple-dyed silk shirt or an Armani suit, if moths infest your closet, then your expensive clothes are no more valuable than ordinary rags.

Second, Jesus mentioned rust, which can destroy (v. 19). The Greek word *brosis* refers to the corrosion of metals. The fact is, a Rolls-Royce, Lamborghini, or Ferrari is just as prone to getting rusted as a Ford, Chevrolet, or Honda. That's just the way of the world. Things break down, get damaged, and can be destroyed—no matter how much money we paid for them.

But *brosis* can also refer to other kinds of decay and destruction. For example, it can refer to something that eats away at a supply of grain. In the predominantly agricultural economy in which Jesus was originally speaking, things like blight, drought, or locusts could be devastating. They still are in many regions of the world. But even if you brought in a bumper harvest, you still had to worry about rats and mildew. Our wealthiest cities today have huge rat populations that feed on the scraps of food thrown out by some of the trendiest and most expensive restaurants in the nation.

Third, if moths, rust, or rats don't ruin our expensive clothes, toys, and food, then Jesus pointed out the possibility we could lose our wealth to "thieves [who] break in and steal" (v. 19). Ancient homes were easy to break into, since they were primarily made of mud brick. Anyone with a sharp tool could dig through a wall and steal your goods. Today, with gated communities, security cameras, motion detectors, and sophisticated locks, it's harder for thieves to break in. Even so, as a security expert told me, if thieves really want to break into your house, they'll find a way in, no matter what security system you've installed.

However, thieves don't always have to carry crowbars. A bad investment or a sharp downturn in the economy can steal your money just as well. And even if your wealth survives after your death, you can't take it with you. Solomon was wise enough to understand this truth: "We all come to the end of our lives as naked and empty-handed as on the day we were born. We can't take our riches with us" (Eccles. 5:15 NLT).[4] When oil tycoon John D. Rockefeller died, his butler was asked how much the old man left behind. He replied, "He left it *all* behind."[5]

This reminds me of the story about an old miser who called together his pastor, lawyer, and doctor just before his death. He said to them, "It's been said you can't take it with you when you go. Hogwash! Here are three envelopes, each containing $100,000. As they are lowering my casket into the grave, I want each of you to throw in those envelopes."

Each agreed and did so when the day came. As the three men walked away from the gravesite, the pastor said, "Gentlemen, I have a confession to make. I didn't throw all the money into the grave. The church has needs, so I took $50,000 and only threw in half." The doctor, feeling guilty, also confessed, "Well, I'm in the process of building a clinic, so I took out $75,000 and only threw in $25,000." The lawyer looked at his two friends with astonishment. "I'm ashamed of you two," he said. "I threw in 100 percent as requested. I wrote him a personal check for the full amount."

Since we can't take it with us, what did Jesus advise? He said, "Store up for yourselves treasures in heaven, where neither moth nor rust destroys, and where thieves do not break in or steal" (Matt. 6:20). Eternal treasures are bug-proof, rust-proof, rat-proof, theft-proof, and depression-proof. So how do we go about investing in heaven?

Earlier in His sermon, Jesus mentioned the rewards that await Christians who are persecuted because of Him (5:12), who love their enemies (v. 46), and who pray and fast in secret (6:6, 18). Some of these rewards include godly character and a clean conscience. But the Bible also speaks of other rewards—or "crowns"—that await those who are faithful during this life:

- The *imperishable* crown is awarded to those who live a Spirit-filled, disciplined life (1 Cor. 9:25).
- The crown of *rejoicing* is awarded to those who dedicate themselves to evangelism and discipleship (1 Thess. 2:19).

- The crown of *righteousness* is awarded to those who long to see Christ's return (2 Tim. 4:8).
- The crown of *life* is awarded to those who endure suffering faithfully (James 1:12).
- The crown of *glory* is awarded to those who serve faithfully as elders and pastors (1 Pet. 5:4).

These rewards all come from the good works Christians perform after they trust in Christ as Savior—not to earn their salvation but as a result of salvation. (As Paul wrote in Ephesians 2:8–10, we are not saved *by* good works but *for* good works.) These "crowns," or rewards, are deposited in the bank of heaven, where they are kept safe and secure until God disperses them at the appointed time.

Jesus capped off this section about treasures by reminding His followers to watch our hearts, saying,

> For where your treasure is, there your heart will be also. (Matt. 6:21)

We tend to move toward whatever object we're looking at. Try this sometime: go for a walk with your spouse or a friend and carry on a conversation. At some point during your walk, don't look at what's in front of you; instead, look at who you're talking to, and see if you don't start to drift closer together. What you look at determines your destination. Or, to paraphrase Jesus, what gleams in your eye guides your heart.

Perhaps it's time to pause for a moment and do some soul-searching. Where is *your* heart when it comes to the topic of your money? Are you more concerned about the things of earth—the next raise, a better car, a bigger house, a dream vacation—than you are the things of heaven? Are you selfish and tightfisted, hoarding what you have instead of giving it for the kingdom of God? Have you acquired enough, or is your attitude like that of Rockefeller, who when asked how much money was enough, supposedly quipped, "Just a little bit more"? Rockefeller's generous contemporary Andrew Carnegie had a different attitude about money. He wrote, "The man who dies rich thus dies disgraced."[6]

Are you content with what God has given you and satisfied with His provision to meet your needs? Do you "set your mind on the things above" (Col. 3:2)? Is God's will for your life—and for your bank account—more important to you than your own? Bible teacher Warren Wiersbe wrote, "What does it mean to lay up treasure in heaven? It means to use *all that we have* for the glory of God."[7]

Two Eyes: Good and Bad

In Matthew 6:22–23, Jesus changed the metaphor from the heart to the eye. He said,

> The eye is the lamp of the body; so then if your eye is clear, your whole body will be full of light. But if your eye is bad, your whole body will be full of darkness. If then the light that is in you is darkness, how great is the darkness!

At first glance, this seems like an unrelated transition to another topic, but it's not. Jesus was bringing our priorities into sharper focus. If we have "clear" sight, then the "whole body will be full of light" (v. 22), meaning we'll see earthly riches for what they really are—false and fleeting. The Greek word for "clear" (*haplous*) means "single, simple, sincere."[8] We should view money with a clear focus, understanding that "money has never made any man rich."[9]

But if we don't see things that way—if we have double vision—then Jesus said we have poor eyesight. "If your eye is bad, your whole body will be full of darkness" (v. 23). If we don't see riches for what they really are, we'll become greedy, envious, and selfish. When we trade the eternal for the temporal, we become spiritually and morally blind. The wise King Solomon put it this way: "A man with an evil eye hastens after wealth and does not know that want will come upon him" (Prov. 28:22).

Two Masters: God and Money

Jesus said we have a choice to make between two treasures, two visions—and two masters. In Matthew 6:24, He said,

> No one can serve two masters; for either he will hate the one and love the other, or he will be devoted to one and despise the other. You cannot serve God and wealth.

To say yes to one master is to say no to the other. There is no third option.

Where will you place your security? Jesus said we can either choose God or choose money. We can't choose both—or a percentage of both, a sort of 60/40 split between God and money. The choice we have to make is all or nothing. Both God and money demand single-minded allegiance.

After Andrew Carnegie made his great wealth, he became disillusioned with the corruption money brought to many of his contemporaries and decided to dedicate his life to philanthropic endeavors. He wrote a small tract titled "The Gospel of Wealth," extolling the virtue of philanthropy. One biographer wrote, "[Carnegie] concluded that life devoted to making money was an unworthy goal. While a man must have an idol . . . money was the worst one imaginable. He decided then that a life devoted solely to making money led to a depraved soul and a loss of one's inner sense of self and humanity."[10]

What's it going to be for you—God or money? The choice is yours to make . . . and it has eternal consequences.

A Word about Worry

In Matthew 6:19–24, Jesus dealt with the *love of money.* Then in verses 25–34, He dealt with *worry because of money.*[11] In this section, Jesus explained that worry is unnecessary, unworthy, and unfruitful.[12]

Worry Is Unnecessary

In verse 25, Jesus made the link between wealth and worry:

> For this reason I say to you, do not be worried about your life, as to what you will eat or what you will drink; nor for your body, as to what you will put on. Is not life more than food, and the body more than clothing?

In other words, Jesus was saying, you can't worry your way to wealth.

You might think you will overcome the temptation of storing up treasures on earth when you've earned enough to take care of your needs. But life has a way of siphoning off our money, leaving in its place anxiety about the future. But Jesus commanded, "Do not be worried about your life" or about the things necessary for life (v. 25).

Whether you're a person of means or struggling to get by, food and clothing are the basics of life; it's just a difference between caviar and cabbage, Gucci and Goodwill. But life is more than the basics we need for survival. That's the point of Jesus's question at the end of verse 25: "Is not life more than food, and the body more than clothing?" Of course it is! Life is about God and conforming our character and conduct to His standards. If we did that, we wouldn't worry.

Whenever we are tempted to worry about money or material things, all we need to do is go outside and observe nature. Jesus continued,

> Look at the birds of the air, that they do not sow, nor reap nor gather into barns, and yet your heavenly Father feeds them. Are you not worth much more than they? (v. 26)

God provides for His creatures—small and great. This doesn't mean we can kick back with a tall glass of lemonade and expect God to bring home our bacon and fry it up too. We have work to do, just as birds have to expend effort to find food. But it doesn't mean we should worry.

Fretting doesn't put food on the table, and it doesn't extend our lives. That's why Jesus asked,

> And who of you by being worried can add a single hour to his life? (v. 27)

You can't worry your way into an extra second in your day, so what makes you think you can worry your way into an extra dollar in your wallet?

Worrying not only doesn't feed you, but it doesn't clothe you either. Jesus said,

> Observe how the lilies of the field grow; they do not toil nor do they spin, yet I say to you that not even Solomon in all his glory clothed himself like one of these. (vv. 28–29)

So why are you worried about clothing? God knows what you need and will make sure you're cared for.

Wildflowers cover the ground and are beautiful, but they last only a short time. Every spring in Texas, where I live, I look forward to seeing the spectacular blooms of bluebonnets that adorn our roadsides, thanks to people who have seeded them along state highways. Many Texans have a tradition of taking family photos in these fields of blooms. Yet they have to hurry—while bluebonnets are our state flower, they bloom only for about six weeks. Yet those bluebonnets don't worry about when their colors will fade or whether they'll come back next year looking like weeds. That's Jesus's point:

> If God so clothes the grass of the field, which is alive today and tomorrow is thrown into the furnace, will He not much more clothe you? You of little faith! (v. 30)

Our problem isn't the smallness of our God but the smallness of our faith. Many who have earthly treasures wring their hands in worry about whether they might lose money.

Many who don't have earthly treasures wring their hands in worry about ways to get money. According to Jesus, both responses are unnecessary.

Worry Is Unworthy

Jesus went on to say that worry is unworthy of those who follow Him because it makes us no better than those who have no faith at all. He said,

> Do not worry then, saying, "What will we eat?" or "What will we drink?" or "What will we wear for clothing?" For the Gentiles eagerly seek all these things. (vv. 31–32)

Jesus was saying, since unbelievers have nothing else to rely on but their own cunning and hard work, they scratch and scrape for every dime they can get and then sit on it like Scrooge, counting their money day and night.

But that's not the attitude Christians should adopt. Jesus explained,

> Your heavenly Father knows that you need all these things. But seek first His kingdom and His righteousness, and all these things will be added to you. (vv. 32–33)

God knows what you need, so there's no need to worry about whether you'll have enough treasure on earth to buy food, drink, and clothing. Instead of seeking the world's goods, seek God's kingdom and righteousness—"and [God] will give you everything you need" (v. 33 NLT).

Remember, *righteousness* as Jesus used it in the Sermon on the Mount isn't about our right standing before God when we place our faith in Christ. Instead, He was talking about right living—pursuing God's standards for our lives. We ought to be spending our waking hours thinking about and going after God's kingdom and His righteousness, not focusing on how we can turn a buck or double our money (which Will Rogers once said was easily done by folding it and putting it back in our pocket).

Jesus promised that those who surpass the righteousness of the scribes and Pharisees (5:20), as well as those who pray and fast earnestly in private (6:6, 18), would be rewarded. What makes you think He won't keep His promise to provide sufficient income to take care of your needs if you're honestly trying to conform your life to His will?

King David wrote, "I have been young and now I am old, yet I have not seen the righteous forsaken or his descendants begging bread" (Ps. 37:25). Because David pursued God's kingdom and righteousness, he never went hungry. Neither did his son Solomon, who echoed his father's words: "The LORD will not allow the righteous to hunger, but He will reject the craving of the wicked" (Prov. 10:3).

You and I have a choice to make. We can either worry about money like the pagans do and carry around the burden of anxiety, or we can pursue God's kingdom and righteousness and see Him work in our lives by providing all that we need to sustain and enjoy life.

Worry Is Unfruitful

Since God has promised to care for our every need, we don't need to worry about how we're going to feed or clothe ourselves; it's simply unfruitful. And this applies not only to our todays but to our tomorrows. Someone has correctly observed, "Worry does not empty tomorrow of its sorrow. It empties today of its strength."[13] That's why Jesus said,

> Do not worry about tomorrow; for tomorrow will care for itself. Each day has enough trouble of its own. (Matt. 6:34)

Remember, He instructed us to pray for our *daily* bread (v. 11), not for tomorrow's bread or next week's bread. God's grace is enough for today, and His grace will be sufficient for tomorrow. So we must learn to live one day at a time.

A Word about Wealth and Worry

When it comes to wealth and worry, the essence of Jesus's message is simple: *you can't worry your way to wealth*. Of course, if a pithy saying like that was all we needed to stop worrying about money, then Jesus could have just said it and saved His breath. But we need a little more than that to apply this message to our lives, so let's refocus our hearts and minds when it comes to money. And there are two practical things we can do today to help ourselves do that.

First, we can *put first things first*. Jesus said it like this: "Seek *first* His kingdom and His righteousness, and all these things will be added to you" (v. 33). How can we do that? Well, look back to the prayer Jesus taught us to pray:

- *Seek to glorify God in our lives*. We learn to "hallow" God's name in our lives (v. 9).
- *Seek God's governance over all of our lives*. We let God rule our lives, just as He rules over His kingdom (v. 10).

- *Seek God's game plan for our lives.* We let God have free rein in our lives (v. 10).

Second, we can *live day by day.* That's what Jesus meant when He said, "Do not worry about tomorrow; for tomorrow will care for itself. Each day has enough trouble of its own" (v. 34). You have responsibilities and obligations to take care of today—bills to pay and groceries to buy. If you don't take care of them today, then they will roll over into tomorrow, which only increases your stress and worry. So don't put it off today, even if you could do it tomorrow.

And whatever you're concerned about, don't leave God out of the equation. The root cause of worrying is calculating your situation without God. Most of our anxious thoughts usually begin with these two words: *What if . . .*

- What if I lose my job?
- What if my mate leaves me for another person?
- What if my child rebels against God?
- What if the stock market crashes?

Whenever you find yourself fixating on a troubling and hypothetical what-if scenario, don't forget to add God to your thinking:

- What if I lose my job, *but God* provides a more fulfilling one?
- What if my mate leaves me for another person, *but God* provides a more loving one?
- What if my child rebels against God, *but God* turns my child's heart back to Himself?

- What if the stock market crashes, *but God* provides for me as He always has?

Don't forget you have a heavenly Father who made you, who loves you, who sent His Son to die for you, and who wants to spend eternity with you. God not only cares about your needs but also can do far and above anything you can imagine.

nine

Straight Talk about
Your Needs

CHILDREN OFTEN GET CONFUSED between their wants and their needs. I remember when our daughters were young, our older daughter would have preferred to have Blue Bell vanilla ice cream for every meal, while our younger daughter insisted she could live on Pop-Tarts! But Amy and I knew that what our girls really *needed* were three healthy meals a day. Children may want to eat junk food all day long, but good parents teach their children the difference between wants and needs, as well as what's appropriate to meet their needs.

Now, as adults, most of us understand our needs. We know we need nutritious food, adequate shelter, and appropriate clothing. But that doesn't mean we *need* caviar, a beach house, or an Armani suit! The hard lesson for us is learning how to be satisfied when our needs are met, even if our wants go unfulfilled.

We carry this same mentality into the spiritual realm. We know we need to be more like Christ, but we want to be more like Christ on our own terms. We don't necessarily want to give up anything. We know we need to do God's will in our lives, but we'd prefer He just rubber-stamp what we want. But as a good Father, God knows what we really need.

In the Sermon on the Mount, Jesus explained that God wants to teach us the hard lesson of being satisfied when He meets our needs.

Two Key Principles

Before Jesus got into His teaching about our wants and needs in Matthew 7, He first laid down two important principles, each as practical today as the day when they were first delivered.

A Principle of Judgment

In verses 1–5, Jesus taught we must be careful when we judge others. He said,

> Do not judge so that you will not be judged. For in the way you judge, you will be judged; and by your standard of measure, it will be measured to you. Why do you look at the speck that is in your brother's eye, but do not notice the log that is in your own eye? Or how can you say to your brother, "Let me take the speck out of your eye," and behold, the log is in your own eye? You hypocrite, first take the log out of your own eye, and then you will see clearly to take the speck out of your brother's eye.

People love to quote verse 1: "Do not judge so that you will not be judged." The popular thinking in our culture today is, *We should never judge people. After all, Jesus said, "Do not judge."* But was Jesus saying that we should never judge anybody for any reason? Not at all. In fact, as we will look at more closely in the next chapter, Jesus later said in this sermon that we are to inspect the attitudes and actions of other Christians to judge whether they are false prophets: "You will know them by their fruits" (v. 16). Over and over, the Bible says we are to judge; we are to make discerning decisions.

So what did Jesus mean when He said don't judge one another? The judgment Jesus was talking about in Matthew 7:1–5 is a pharisaical judgment. The Pharisees loved to condemn people and say, "This person is beyond redemption." We're never to say that. Only God can perform that kind of judgment.

But there is a righteous type of judgment. It's a merciful thing to help somebody remove a speck from their eye, to help them deal with a sin in order to become more like Christ. Jesus was saying that if you really want to help a fellow Christian, make sure you've first dealt with the log in your own eye—the sin in your own life—so you can see clearly to help somebody else. That doesn't mean you have to be perfect. But if there is some glaring sin in your life you haven't dealt with, you are not going to be able to perform spiritual surgery on somebody else. Think about a surgeon who begins a procedure by blindfolding him- or herself. Neither the surgeon nor the patient would feel very confident in that situation, would they? In the same way, if we don't deal with sin in our own lives, we're not going to be in any position to help other people.

A Principle of Evangelism

In verse 6, Jesus said we must be discerning when sharing the gospel:

> Do not give what is holy to dogs, and do not throw your pearls before swine, or they will trample them under their feet, and turn and tear you to pieces.

Notice that this verse also requires you to make a judgment. You have to decide who's a dog or a swine and who is not—who is hard-hearted and unworthy of casting your pearls before and who is open to the gospel.

Some Christians use Matthew 7:6 as an excuse not to share the gospel with anyone. But a failure to evangelize discloses our lack of discernment between those who are receptive and those who are not. No wonder Jesus went on to address our need to pray for God's help in verses 7–11. Of all the needs we have, none is greater than our need for God to empower us to live in a way that reflects the person of Christ.

Problems with Prayer

When it comes to praying for God to meet our needs, many of us encounter one of two problems. First, *we believe prayer to be unnecessary, unproductive, or both, so we don't pray.* As D. A. Carson pointed out, "Genuine Christians in the West are not characterized by prayer. Our environment loves hustle and bustle, smooth organization and powerful institutions, human self-confidence and human achievement, new opinions and novel schemes; and the church of Jesus Christ has conformed so thoroughly to this environment that it is often difficult to see how it differs in these matters from contemporary paganism. . . . Our low spiritual ebb is directly traceable to the flickering feebleness of our prayers."[1]

Second, *we believe things about God that aren't true.* Jesus said in Matthew 7:7–8, "Ask, and it will be given to you; seek, and you will find; knock, and it will be opened to you. For everyone who asks receives, and he who seeks finds, and to him who knocks it will be opened." Many see Jesus's words here as a blanket promise for anything they want—a blank check signed by Jesus and cashable in heaven. All we need to do is fill in the amount.

I hate to disappoint you, but that's not the case. In the words of a friend, God isn't "a divine candy machine dispensing blessings at the push of a button."[2] But He is happy to answer us if we pray according to His will, as the apostle John wrote, "This is the confidence which we have before Him, that, if we ask anything *according to His will*, He hears us" (1 John 5:14). You and I can pray confidently about specific concerns, knowing that if that answer is within the will of God, He will answer it.

Now, adding the qualifier "if it is according to Your will" to our prayers is not some sort of cop-out. It is also not meant to let God off the hook. God's will is a wonderful, protective fence He has placed around every one of His children—not to keep good things from entering our lives but to keep harmful things out of them.

As I look back over my prayer journals from decades ago, I'm honestly more grateful for God's "no" answers to my prayer requests than His affirmative answers! I wasn't necessarily grateful at the time, but I'm very grateful now.

In the context of the Sermon on the Mount in Matthew 7, God's will is that we ask Him to help us navigate the difficulties of life. God's ear is always attentive to those who come to Him in prayer, but only if we are more concerned about His glory than our own self-centered desires. "You do not have because you do not ask," James wrote. "You ask and do not receive, because you ask with wrong motives, so that you may spend it on your pleasures" (4:2–3).

Of course, there are other reasons that God might not hear your prayers. Here are just some of the reasons He may choose to ignore or deny your requests:

- You're not praying from a pure heart (Ps. 66:18).
- You're not praying in faith (James 1:5–8).
- You're not praying while living obediently (1 John 3:22).
- You're not praying in order to bring glory to God (1 Cor. 10:31).
- You're not praying with an attitude of humility (Luke 18:9–14).
- You're not praying with sensitivity to the Holy Spirit (Eph. 6:18).[3]

Principles of Powerful Praying

With the problems of prayer in mind, let's look at Matthew 7:7–8 and discover some practical principles of prayer. Jesus said,

Ask, and it will be given to you; seek, and you will find; knock, and it will be opened to you. For everyone who asks receives, and he who seeks finds, and to him who knocks it will be opened.

Each of these verbs—ask, seek, and knock—is a present imperative, meaning we ought to always do what is commanded. We should read them as, "Keep on asking . . . keep on seeking . . . keep on knocking." I see two principles implied in these commands.

First of all, *we are to pray with persistence.* The apostle Paul told the believers at Thessalonica to "pray without ceasing" (1 Thess. 5:17). That applies to us as well. This isn't the mindless mumblings Jesus warned against in Matthew 6:7 but heartfelt petitions of a soul in need. What have you been asking for, seeking after, and knocking about in prayer? Have you given up because the Lord didn't answer your prayer immediately? Or are you still at it, asking persistently, seeking consistently, and knocking insistently?

This persistent asking makes me think back again to when our daughters were young. Whenever one or both of our girls wanted or needed something, they might ask Amy about it. If she didn't respond straightaway, they would track me down and ask me. And if I put them off, they *kept asking*. If they happened to come home and couldn't find either one of us but had something to ask for, they would track us down like heat-seeking missiles. And if they didn't find us immediately, they *kept seeking*. Then there were those times when their needs or wants had to take a back seat to something Amy and I were dealing with at the moment. In order to address a more pressing issue, we might go into our bedroom or my study and close the door. Of course, that didn't mean the girls walked away; they *kept knocking*.

Moms and dads sometimes need a break from the incessant asking of children, which is why a mother posted this note on the bathroom door:

Attention Children:
The bathroom door is closed. Please do not stand here and talk, whine, or ask questions. Wait until I get out. Yes, it is locked. I want it that way. It is not broken. I am not trapped. I know I have left it unlocked, and even open at times, since you were born, because I was afraid some horrible tragedy might occur while I was in there, but it's been ten years and I want some PRIVACY. Do not ask me how long I will be. I will come out when I am done. Do not bring the phone to the bathroom door. Do not go running back to the phone yelling, "She's in the BATHROOM!" Do not begin to fight as soon as I go in. Do not stick your little fingers under the door and wiggle them. Do not slide pennies, LEGOs, or notes under the door. Even when you were two this got a little tiresome. If you have followed me down the hall talking, and are still talking as you face this closed door, please turn around, walk away, and wait for me in another room. I will be glad to listen to you when I am done. And yes, I still love you.

Signed,
Mom[4]

The Lord never needs to close the door and post such a note. He neither slumbers nor sleeps, Psalm 121:4 assures us. So keep asking, keep seeking, keep knocking. Pray with persistence.

Second, *we are to pray with passion.* Whatever request you're bringing before the Lord, have you been bold without being obnoxious? "Don't bargain with God," reads Eugene Peterson's paraphrase of Matthew 7:7–8 in *The Message.* "Be direct. Ask for what you need. This isn't a cat-and-mouse, hide-and-seek game we're in." If you earnestly seek the Lord's will and genuinely ask Him to intervene on your behalf, then you'll receive what you ask for, find what you've been looking for, and gain access to the places you've longed to go. But you must keep at it—and mean it.

Passion for something is a sure motivator for persistence. Paul said in Galatians 6:9, "Let us not lose heart in doing good, for in due time we will reap if we do not grow weary." What greater good could you do than to talk with the Lord about your needs or the needs of others? E. M. Bounds said prayer involves passion. "Desire gives fervor to prayer," he wrote. "Strong desires make strong prayers."[5]

In His sermon, Jesus already gave us a model for how to pray in what has become known as the Lord's Prayer (Matt. 6:9–13). What we need to do now is to put into practice what He taught us. And there's nothing greater to pray about than whatever needs we or our loved ones have today. Pray tirelessly and passionately until God has answered you, revealed His will to you, or opened a door of opportunity for you—even if you have to wear a hole in the carpet until He does.

Answers: Stones and Snakes

Jesus emphasized that God hears our prayers when we come to Him with a legitimate need (not necessarily a want) by offering two illustrations of how a loving father meets the needs of his children. He said,

> What man is there among you who, when his son asks for a loaf, will give him a stone? Or if he asks for a fish, he will not give him a snake, will he? (Matt. 7:9–10)[6]

The seashores of Israel are covered in round stones that look exactly like little loaves of bread. But no good father would offer those to his child because the stones are inedible and could crack the child's teeth.

Never once when my girls were little and asked for a peanut butter and jelly sandwich did I give them a peanut butter and jelly*fish* sandwich. This doesn't mean Amy and I didn't have to help our girls learn to eat healthy foods they didn't particularly like. But what good parent doesn't do that?

My own mother tried to get me to eat green beans when I was a boy—a vegetable that, in my opinion, ranked somewhere below boiled spinach. I preferred broccoli, so instead of forcing me to eat green beans, my mother would serve me broccoli. What she didn't do was give me a plate of earthworms in place of green beans. (If she had, I'm not sure they would have tasted any worse to me!) That's the point Jesus was making: if a child asks for what is good and necessary, like bread or fish, no father in his right mind would give his child a stone or snake as a substitute.

Jesus then contrasted our response to our children when they ask for good things with God's response to His children when we ask for good things:

If you then, being evil, know how to give good gifts to your children, how much more will your Father who is in heaven give what is good to those who ask Him! (v. 11)

Don't read more into the word "evil" than necessary. Jesus was making a comparison between good parents and the best Parent—God the Father. Compared to God, who is the very definition of goodness, we aren't so good. We might have come to faith in Christ, receiving forgiveness of our sins, but our sin nature is still alive and active. We're sinning saints who are still in need of forgiveness. If we weren't, there would be no reason for 1 John 1:9: "If we confess our sins, He is faithful and righteous to forgive us our sins and to cleanse us from all unrighteousness." Besides, Isaiah 64:6 says, "All our righteous deeds are like a filthy garment." So, by comparison, even our best is evil next to God's goodness.

The stark difference between God and human beings makes Matthew 7:11 all the more encouraging. If our self-centered natures would never think of giving our children counterfeits when they have genuine needs, *how much more* will our heavenly Father, who is pure goodness, give His children good gifts when we ask? This "how much more" comparison should thrill every child of God and motivate us to rush boldly and regularly to God's throne with our requests!

The parallel passage in Luke 11 specifies that the greatest good and need we should ask God to give us is the gift of the Holy Spirit (v. 13), who is given to all those who place their faith in Christ. Christian philosopher Peter Kreeft was right: "Only one thing in life is guaranteed: not happiness, not the pursuit of happiness, not liberty, not even life. The only thing

189

we are absolutely guaranteed is the only thing we absolutely need: God."[7] The Holy Spirit helps us to know what to pray for, and He prays for us. Paul said, "The Spirit . . . helps our weakness; for we do not know how to pray as we should, but the Spirit Himself intercedes for us with groanings too deep for words; and He who searches the hearts knows what the mind of the Spirit is, because He intercedes for the saints according to the will of God" (Rom. 8:26–27).

God is overjoyed to give Himself when we ask, seek, and knock, just as Jeremiah 29:13 promises: "You will seek Me and find Me when you search for Me with all your heart."

The Lord gives other good gifts besides the Holy Spirit. The Bible tells us He gives wisdom to those who lack it (James 1:5), opportunities to share the gospel (Col. 4:2–4), and greater faith to those who ask for it (Luke 17:5–6). And anytime you ask for, seek after, and knock about personal spiritual growth, God is always ready to answer.

The Golden Rule

By the time we get to Matthew 7:12, we've reached the climax of Jesus's sermon. Bible commentator William Barclay said, "This is probably the most universally famous thing that Jesus ever said. With this commandment, the Sermon on the Mount reaches its summit. . . . It is the topmost peak of social ethics, and the Everest of all ethical teaching."[8]

This is Jesus's summary statement of the Sermon on the Mount:

> In everything, therefore, treat people the same way you want them to treat you, for this is the Law and the Prophets. (v. 12)[9]

Jesus made another statement summarizing the essence of the Old Testament when He said, "You shall love the Lord your God with all your heart, and with all your soul, and with all your mind." This is the great and foremost commandment. The second is like it, "You shall love your neighbor as yourself" (22:37–39).

The "Golden Rule," as Matthew 7:12 has become known, focuses on the second commandment, providing a specific application of how we can demonstrate love for our neighbor.[10] Jesus didn't need to lay out a separate principle focusing on the love of God, because we cannot love our neighbor or do what is good and necessary for them without first loving God.

The basic principle of the Golden Rule wasn't unique to Jesus. Confucius, Greek philosophers, and Jewish rabbis had taught something similar before Jesus's time. However, what was unique is that Jesus stated the principle positively; the others stated it negatively. "Don't do to others what you don't want done to you," is how they put it.[11]

Jesus turned this idea on its head and placed the emphasis on others, saying, "Do to others whatever you would like them to do to you" (NLT). The others before Jesus said, "It's okay to be passive." But Jesus said, "You must be active." There's a world of difference between saying, "I must not hurt someone because I don't want to be hurt," and "I must go out of my way to help someone because I might need help someday." The law compels the one, but love compels the other.

The Golden Rule is a fitting conclusion of the first eleven verses in Matthew 7. Treating people the way we would like to be treated means we don't judge them harshly or unjustly (vv. 1–5), we don't turn people off to the gospel by ramming it down their throats before they're ready to listen (v. 6), and we lift up the needs of others before God in prayer in the same way we hope they are bringing our needs before God (vv. 7–11).

Application: Needs and Wants

Wanting what meets your needs, not necessarily your desires, is a hard lesson to learn. It only comes by developing a deeper relationship with God. And one of the best ways to do that is through the practice of prayer. So let me give you three principles to help you get started today.

First, *pray persistently and passionately*. Be relentless in your prayers, continuing to ask, seek, and knock. The assurance and encouragement of Jesus's promise in Matthew 7:7–11 is that God will answer when we persistently and passionately ask for, seek after, and knock about what is good for us, whether it meets a material or a spiritual need.

Do you need the necessities of life: food, shelter, or clothing? Tell God what you need, and don't stop until you get it. Then be sure to thank Him. Keep in mind, though, that He might not provide for your lavish wants but will make sure you are provided for. Do you need a job? Knock on God's door—and keep knocking. He'll open a door of opportunity for you to work and make enough money to take care of your needs and the needs of your family.

Maybe your deepest need is spiritual, since we are all spiritual beings. If you're sick of your sin, then ask God to forgive you and create in you a new life that can only be found through faith in the death and resurrection of Jesus. God never says no to those prayers.

Maybe you're already a believer, but you've been struggling with sin. Be relentless in asking Him for strength to resist temptation and to choose holiness. If you have a lying tongue, ask God to help you speak truth. If you have a critical spirit, ask God to replace it with grace. If you're a tightwad, ask God to open your hands and help you be generous. Whatever will make your attitudes and actions reflect Jesus, ask for it, seek it out, and knock on the door until God answers.

Second, *seek after what God wants and surrender your will to His.* As we pray over days, weeks, months, and maybe even years—for a wayward child who has left the faith, a chronic illness, a hard-hearted family member, a financial need, or a difficulty in the church—God often uses the passage of time and the persistence of our prayers to change us before He changes our situation. We find our hearts becoming softer, our wills bending, and our lives conforming to His desires more than our own. Danish philosopher Søren Kierkegaard wrote, "Prayer does not change God, but it changes the one who prays."[12] The more you surrender to God's will, the more you'll discover that what you want matches up with what He wants.

Third, *pray for your needs, but also pray for the needs of others.* Many of us know the Golden Rule by heart. Now it's time to put it into practice. We have needs, but so do others, and we should be asking God to meet their needs. To put it in the formula of the Golden Rule: pray for the needs of others in the same way you want others to pray for your needs.

Samuel Johnson was famous for his English dictionary. A devout man, he was overheard praying one morning: "Almighty God, the giver of all good things, without whose help all labor is ineffectual, and without whose grace all wisdom is folly, grant, I beseech Thee, that in this undertaking Thy Holy Spirit may not be withheld from me, but that I may promote Thy glory, and the salvation of myself and others; grant this, O Lord, for the sake of Thy Son, Jesus Christ. Amen."[13]

That's not a bad summary of what Jesus taught in His Sermon on the Mount about praying for our needs.

Go to God in prayer regularly and seek His will. Continually ask Him, seek His face, and knock on His door with your requests for His provision for you and others. And in the process, God will transform your desires so that what you *want* is what you really *need*.

ten

Straight Talk about Your Eternal Destiny

PRESIDENTIAL SPEECHWRITER AND OPINION COLUMNIST Peggy Noonan attended the state funeral for president Ronald Reagan. Surrounded by other members of President Reagan's administration, she jotted down some observations of those present. Each person, she noted, had to make hard decisions about life. Of Jeane Kirkpatrick, who'd served as Reagan's ambassador to the United Nations, Peggy wrote, "Somewhere along the way, I have always felt, she made a decision. She chose to follow the academic and analytical part of her nature . . . and not perhaps other parts of her inner self, parts perhaps less definitive and constructive and perhaps more merry." Peggy then concluded, "Life is options up to a point, and then it's decisions made."[1]

As my daughters were growing up, I taught them, "To say yes to one thing is to say no to other things." That's what Peggy Noonan meant about options and decisions. If the Lord hadn't called me into the ministry when I was fifteen years old, I probably would have studied broadcasting or finance and would be working professionally in one of those fields today. Although the Lord has been gracious enough to allow me to use these two passions in my ministry, saying yes to the one thing I knew God was calling me to do meant saying no to other viable options in my life.

We all have turning points in our lives when we must choose between competing choices. Most of life is made up of insignificant choices—what to eat for lunch, what to wear, or where to go on vacation. A few choices are more significant: which university to attend, which car to purchase, or which job to accept. However, some decisions are life-altering, such as whether to get married and to whom, and whether to have children and how many.

Peggy is right: "Life is options up to a point, and then it's decisions made." Whatever decisions you make (or have made) concerning significant life events such as your career or marital status or family are insignificant compared to the most important decision you'll ever make: where you will reside for eternity.

One Fate, Two Destinations

Unfortunately, you and I don't get to choose whether or not we will die. The fact is, not one of us gets out of this world alive. In Ecclesiastes 9:2, Solomon said, "It is the same for all. There is one fate for the righteous and for the wicked; for the good, for the clean and for the unclean; for the man who offers a sacrifice and for the one who does not sacrifice." In other words, it doesn't matter whether you're good or bad, righteous or unrighteous, a believer or an unbeliever—there is one fate for everybody, and that is death. We are all going to die someday.

Although we all have one fate, there are two different eternal destinations: heaven and hell. In Matthew 25:46, Jesus described our two possible destinations when we die. Referring to the unrighteous, He said, "These will go away into eternal punishment, but the righteous into eternal life."

You see, death is not the end. You and I are going to live forever, regardless of what we believe about God. The Bible says we are eternal beings. It's the *location* of our eternity that makes the difference. Some will spend eternity in heaven with God while others will spend eternity in hell, but everybody's going to live forever.

Where do you want to spend eternity? You might say, "I don't have to decide right now. I can put that off until tomorrow." No, you really can't. Not to decide is to decide. Besides, you are not guaranteed tomorrow. The Bible says, "You do not know what your life will be like tomorrow. You are just a vapor that appears for a little while and then vanishes away" (James 4:14). This is why Paul wrote, "Indeed, the 'right time' is now. Today is the day of salvation" (2 Cor. 6:2 NLT).

So you have a decision to make. Where do you want to spend eternity? You can either accept Jesus or reject Him. You'll either enter the kingdom of heaven or enter the kingdom of hell. There's no third alternative, which makes this the most consequential decision you'll make in your life.

It's the choice between eternal blessing or eternal suffering, heaven or hell.

Fortunately, Jesus helped us make this decision in His concluding point in the Sermon on the Mount. These verses serve as the application of His message, because the choice we make today regarding our eternal life will forever affect our tomorrow.

Jesus laid out this choice with four illustrations:

- *Two paths*—the narrow one that leads to life and the wide one that leads to destruction (Matt. 7:13–14).
- *Two trees*—the one that produces good fruit and the one that produces bad fruit (vv. 15–20).
- *Two followers*—the true disciple who does the will of God and the false disciple who pays lip service to God (vv. 21–23).
- *Two houses*—the one built on solid rock and the one built on sand (vv. 24–27).

Two Paths

When I was in the eighth grade, I was required to memorize a poem by Robert Frost titled "The Road Not Taken." Every time I read Matthew 7, I still recall those famous lines that describe a traveler who comes upon two roads—and chooses to take the path less traveled.[2]

Either we can follow the beaten path traveled by many and live ordinary lives, or we can follow the path traveled by few and live extraordinary lives. Though Frost was describing a traveler's journey here on earth, his words are just as applicable to the choice each of us has to make about our eternal destination.

It's the "narrow" path that leads to eternal life in heaven. That's what Jesus was talking about in Matthew 7:13–14:

> Enter through the narrow gate; for the gate is wide and the way is broad that leads to destruction, and there are many who enter through it. For the gate is small and the way is narrow that leads to life, and there are few who find it.

Many laugh at the idea that there's only one path to heaven. But it's true. And that path is only through faith in Jesus Christ, by believing He died for *your* sins when He was crucified, by believing His death paid the penalty *you* should have paid for your sins, and by believing He rose again from the dead and gives *you* new life. Jesus Christ alone is your only hope of salvation.

In John 14:6, Jesus said, "I am *the* way, and *the* truth, and *the* life; no one comes to the Father but through Me." There's nothing ambiguous about that statement. Jesus is not one among several ways to heaven. He is the *one* and *only* way to heaven. There aren't many roads to God. There's one way—and one way only—and that is through Jesus Christ.[3]

Over the years, I've appeared on a number of talk shows. Sometimes the host will tell me, "You're being intolerant when you say Christianity is the only right religion." When people accuse me of being intolerant, I used to respond by pointing out that I was simply quoting the beliefs of the founder of my faith, Jesus Christ. "If you've got a problem," I would say, "then take it up with Him!"

But over the years, I've changed my approach a little by adding, "And the reason He said that is not because He hates us but because He loves us." I now drive that truth home by adding this illustration: "Suppose you awakened in the middle of the night to discover your house was on fire and all the available exits were blocked. Just when you had resigned yourself that you were going to die, a firefighter burst into your bedroom and yelled, 'Follow me; there is one way out of the house!' Would you accuse that firefighter of being intolerant because he insisted there was only one way to escape the flames? Of course not! You would follow him, and you would thank him. Similarly, the only reason Jesus declared there is just one way to escape the flames of hell is because there *is* only one way. Jesus's motivation for urging us to follow Him to safety is not because He hates us but because He loves us."

Jesus said the narrow path to heaven is difficult to find, and few find it. Other theories about heaven might be appealing, easy, and popular, but they're also wrong and lead to ruin. Jesus said the broad path that many people are on "leads to destruction"—eternal death in hell (7:13). Paul made the same point in Philippians 3: "Many walk . . . [who] are enemies of the cross of Christ, whose end is destruction, whose god is their appetite, and whose glory is in their shame, who set their minds on earthly things" (vv. 18–19).

Jesus didn't teach universalism—the belief that everyone will go to heaven. Nor did He subscribe to pluralism—the belief that there are many paths leading to God that are equally legitimate as long as a person is sincere. Both universalism and pluralism appear to be logical, but appearances can be deceiving. Solomon observed, "There is a way which seems right to a man, but its end is the way of death" (Prov. 14:12).

Jesus's point may be difficult to accept, but it is clear: few will be saved and enter heaven, while many will perish and enter hell. Why? Because few are willing to walk the narrow way of following Jesus that leads to the narrow gate of salvation. Instead, they prefer to walk the wide way that leads to the wide gate of destruction.[4] It's like the cartoon I saw with two booths, a person sitting at each one. Above each booth is a sign. A long line forms in front of one booth, but no one is standing in front of the other booth. The sign that has attracted the crowd reads "Comforting Lies." The sign that has not attracted anyone reads "Unpleasant Truths."[5]

One of Satan's most dangerous lies is that you can believe whatever you want to believe and live however you want to live, and everything will turn out okay in the end. The truth is more difficult: if you want to spend eternity in heaven, then you must walk the narrow way by becoming a follower of Christ. But many go on believing a lie, hoping Jesus's pronouncement of destruction isn't really true.

Yet it is true—and it's always been true. In the Old Testament, before the Israelites entered the promised land, the Lord said to them, "I have set before you life and death, the blessing and the curse. So choose life in order that you may live, you and your descendants" (Deut. 30:19). After they entered the land, Joshua laid a similar choice before them: "Choose for yourselves today whom you will serve. . . . As for me and my house, we will serve the LORD" (Josh. 24:15). And after the Israelites were thrown out of the land for choosing to serve other gods, the Lord gave them another chance, saying, "Behold, I set before you the way of life and the way of death" (Jer. 21:8).

In His sermon, Jesus set the same choice before us: Will you choose life through the narrow gate by the narrow way of faith in Jesus Christ, or death through the wide gate by the wide way?

Two Trees

Jesus introduced His next illustration about our eternal destiny with a warning about false prophets:

> Beware of the false prophets, who come to you in sheep's clothing, but inwardly are ravenous wolves. (Matt. 7:15)[6]

Most people who walk the wide path and enter through the wide gate do so because some teacher, author, or preacher left a trail of easy-to-believe lies, and they followed it down the wrong path.

Like wolves dressed in sheep's clothing, false teachers use others for their own self-serving ends. And the best way to identify them is by looking at their actions and attitudes—or, as Jesus phrased it,

> You will know them by their fruits. (v. 16)

True preachers produce refreshing fruit, while false preachers produce rotten fruit. By examining a person's actions and attitudes, we can conclude whether that person's character is good or evil. As Jesus put it,

> Grapes are not gathered from thorn bushes nor figs from thistles, are they? So every good tree bears good fruit, but

the bad tree bears bad fruit. A good tree cannot produce bad fruit, nor can a bad tree produce good fruit. (vv. 17–18)

You don't have to be a horticulturist to know this is true. Jesus explained, "Grapes are not gathered from thorn bushes," but from grapevines. And "figs [are not gathered] from thistles, are they?" (v. 16). No, they're gathered from fig trees. Everyone knows this, but it can sometimes be hard to detect the real from the phony. The buckthorn bush in Israel grew berries that looked like grapes from a distance. And there was a thistle whose flower looked like a fig from a distance. But there was no mistaking a buckthorn berry for a grape when making a PB&J sandwich. And there was no mistaking a thistle flower for a fig when making preserves. That's why Jesus said, "So every good tree bears good fruit, but the bad tree bears bad fruit" (v. 17).

Let's apply this standard to false teachers who claim to represent Christ but don't. What does "fruit" mean when it comes to their teaching and actions? If they teach things that sound good but don't square with the Word of God, then they're false teachers. For example, anyone who preaches that God's primary purpose in your life is that you always experience health and financial prosperity is probably also selling oceanfront property in Arizona! God's purpose is for you to choose faith in Jesus and follow Him. That's the good news and the good fruit. Anything else is rotten to the core.

All of us need to be more like the Berean Christians in Acts 17. The apostle Paul showed up in their city, flashed his credentials as an apostle, and began preaching. The Bereans, who were "noble-minded" (v. 11), said, "Just a minute there, sonny. Before you go any further, we're going to check you out." How did they do that? The Bible says they measured Paul's words against the standard of Scripture.

No matter who stands before you and claims to speak God's message (including yours truly), no matter the number of impressive degrees on their wall or letters after their name, no matter how charming they appear or how beautiful their facilities look, take the time to examine the Scriptures for yourself. It's the squeeze-and-sniff test you should apply to the spiritual fruit produced by every teacher of God's Word. This is why John admonished us, "Beloved, do not believe every spirit, but test the spirits to see whether they are from God, because many false prophets have gone out into the world" (1 John 4:1).

One of the telltale signs of rotten religious teaching is the practice of not offending anyone. False teachers want to make everyone feel good, even if people are on the path to hell. They avoid saying that salvation is by grace alone through faith alone in Christ alone. They steer clear of words like *crucifixion, resurrection, sin, repentance, obedience, discipleship, doctrine, judgment,* and *holiness.* They place an unusual emphasis on love. But it's a love without a direct object, like the person of Christ or His Word; it's more akin to the Beatles' song "All You Need Is Love"—love, love, love. One man who was saved from such teaching said, "Those folks would have loved me right into hell."[7]

Like those who reject Jesus's call to discipleship (the narrow way) and choose to follow their own desires (the wide way), so the rotten fruit of false preachers leads to destruction. In the words of Jesus,

Every tree that does not bear good fruit is cut down and thrown into the fire [of hell]. (Matt. 7:19)

Jesus concluded,

So then, you will know them by their fruits. (v. 20)

Two Followers

False teachers always produce false followers, which is why Jesus targeted them next.

In Christian circles, we tend to put more emphasis on what people say than on what they do. If someone claims to be a follower of Jesus and uses the right Christianese phrases, we tend to believe them without looking too hard to see whether they are actually walking their talk. As a friend of mine says, "You can't say you're going to heaven and live like hell." He doesn't mean Christians don't sin. They certainly do. What he means is that in the long run, those who are truly going to heaven reveal it by their lives—the fruit they produce.

The same is true for those truly going to hell. You may know the old children's vacation Bible school song "If You're Happy and You Know It." It's the one about clapping your hands and stomping your feet. I've taught it to my triplet grandchildren, who sing it with great gusto! It's a silly song, but there's a line in the chorus that's full of theological truth, especially applied to your relationship with Christ: "If you're happy and you know it, then your life will surely show it." True believers do more than believe; they live what they believe in obedience to God's will, as revealed in God's Word.

Jesus said something similar in verse 21:

> Not everyone who says to Me, "Lord, Lord," will enter the kingdom of heaven, but he who does the will of My Father who is in heaven will enter.

To me, those are some of the most terrifying words in the New Testament. Jesus was saying that on the broad path that leads to hell are many people who claim to be Christians. Hell won't just be populated with unrepentant murderers, rapists, and drug dealers but also with religious people, even people who have deceived themselves into thinking they are Christians. That's because simply saying Jesus is Lord doesn't necessarily make you a true believer, not if there hasn't been a transference of your spirit from darkness to light.

The apostle Paul said in Ephesians 5:8–10, "You were formerly darkness, but now you are Light in the Lord; walk as children of Light (for the fruit of the Light consists in all goodness and righteousness and truth), trying to learn what is pleasing to the Lord."

And what exactly is pleasing to the Lord? Jesus taught in the Sermon on the Mount the following things, which reveal the will of God:

- Practicing the Beatitudes.
- Doing all you can to align your character and conduct with God's standards.
- Praying and giving with humility and integrity.
- Making heavenly rewards more important than earthly success.

- Learning to be more gracious and less judgmental.
- Practicing discernment.
- Being persistent in prayer.

Now, I am not preaching a gospel based on works. What I'm saying is this: *only those who have truly come to faith in Jesus Christ can do the will of God.* That's what Jesus implied in Matthew 7:21 when He said, "He who does the will of My Father who is in heaven will enter" the kingdom. It's true that you ought to "confess with your mouth Jesus as Lord," as Paul instructed in Romans 10:9, but you must also "believe in your heart that God raised Him from the dead." Only then, Paul said, "you will be saved."

D. A. Carson made this connection clear: "It is true . . . that no man enters the kingdom because of his obedience; but it is equally true that no man enters the kingdom who is not obedient. It is true that men are saved by God's grace through faith in Christ; but it is equally true that God's grace in a man's life inevitably results in obedience."[8]

Perhaps this illustration will help. Suppose one crisp day in early fall, I invite you to come into my backyard and see my beautiful apple tree. When you look at it, you notice there is not an apple in sight. Instead, the branches are dried up. You try to be diplomatic and say, "I'm afraid your apple tree is sick—it might even be dead." I am incensed and say, "How could you say such a judgmental thing?" You gently reply, "Well, there are no apples on your apple tree." I respond, "Oh, you're right! Wait just a moment." Then I run to the supermarket down the street, purchase some apples, return, and tie them on to the dead branches of my dead apple tree. "There you go! Now my tree is alive!" I say confidently.

No, tying apples to a dead apple tree does not make an apple tree alive, any more than attaching good works to someone who is spiritually dead makes that person spiritually alive. Good works do not produce spiritual life, but they prove there is spiritual life. And where there is no fruit, there is no faith. James, the half brother of Jesus, wrote, "Even so, faith, if it has no works, is dead, being by itself" (2:17).

The day is coming when Jesus will judge false followers—those who merely confess, "Lord, Lord" but didn't make Jesus Lord of their lives by coming to Him in faith. He put it like this in Matthew 7:22–23:

> Many will say to Me on that day, "Lord, Lord, did we not prophesy in Your name, and in Your name cast out demons, and in Your name perform many miracles?" And then I will declare to them, "I never knew you; depart from Me, you who practice lawlessness."

You may be saying, "Wait a minute, Pastor! You said only those who come to faith in Jesus can do the will of God. So how can anyone prophesy, cast out demons, or do miracles without being a true follower of Jesus?" First, let me point out that these false followers *claimed* to have done these things. Jesus didn't say their claims were verified. For all we know, they faked or exaggerated their good works. I have been in ministry for a long time and have seen plenty of phony-baloney "supernatural" works.

Second, let me present to you Exhibit A of a fake follower of Christ: Judas Iscariot. As one of the original twelve disciples, Judas was given "authority over unclean spirits, to cast them out, and to heal every kind of disease and every kind of sickness" (Matt. 10:1) in the name of Christ. Yet Judas was never a true follower of Jesus. He was a thief (John 12:6) and a traitor (18:2). And at one point, Judas was possessed by Satan himself (Luke 22:3).

Paul described this kind of deceptive follower of Christ when he wrote, "Such men are false apostles, deceitful workers, disguising themselves as apostles of Christ. No wonder, for even Satan disguises himself as an angel of light. Therefore, it is not surprising if his servants also disguise themselves as servants of righteousness, whose end will be according to their deeds" (2 Cor. 11:13–15).

Casting out demons and performing miracles are good works, as are fasting and praying. But the quality of those works, like the quality of a person's fruit, is not judged by what appears on the outside but by what's on the inside. An apple might look delicious until you bite into it.

Since Matthew 7:22–23 refers to Jesus's judgment on false followers, we can trust He knows what's going on inside the hearts and minds of those who call Him Lord and claim good works. Scripture reminds us, "God sees not as man sees, for man looks at the outward appearance, but the LORD looks at the heart" (1 Sam. 16:7). Jesus sees every heart and weighs every motive, and He is able to discern the true followers who will enter heaven and the false followers who will enter hell.

Two Houses

In Matthew 7:24–27, Jesus contrasted those who only hear His instructions with those who hear *and obey* His instructions. He said,

Therefore everyone who hears these words of Mine *and acts on them*, may be compared to a wise man who built his house on the rock. And the rain fell, and the floods came, and the winds blew and slammed against that house; and yet it did not fall, for it had been founded on the rock. (vv. 24–25)

In contrast to the house built on rock, there is another house built on sand. Jesus continued,

Everyone who hears these words of Mine *and does not act on them*, will be like a foolish man who built his house on the sand. The rain fell, and the floods came, and the winds blew and slammed against that house; and it fell—and great was its fall. (vv. 26–27)

When you look at these houses, they both appear safe and secure. But the test to see if a house has a strong structure and is watertight is to throw a storm at it. In the fable of "The Three Little Pigs," the one that built a house out of brick instead of straw or sticks is the wise one. So are people who build their lives on the solid foundation of Jesus Christ by putting His words into practice. In contrast, foolish people build their lives on the sandy foundation of anything other than Christ by refusing to obey His words. The apostle James made this same point: "Prove yourselves *doers* of the word, and not merely *hearers* who delude themselves" (1:22).[9]

There's no escaping the storms that come in life. As Job said, "Man, who is born of woman, is short-lived and full of turmoil" (14:1). When storms come into our lives, they reveal the true nature of our faith. If we have built our lives on the strong foundation of Jesus Christ and His Word, the hope of heaven never washes us out to sea. But those who build their lives on some other foundation don't have that hope, and when storms lash and thrash, in time their faithlessness crumbles and destruction comes.

What Choice Will You Make?

We've come to the end of Jesus's Sermon on the Mount, and we have a choice to make. Either we believe Jesus is the Son of God who died on a cross to save us from our sin and rose from the dead to give us eternal life, or we believe Jesus is a fine moral teacher who died at some point in history and is still in His grave. To believe the one is to ensure an eternity in heaven; to believe the other is to ensure an eternity in hell.

That's the whole point of the last sixteen verses of Jesus's sermon. The *two paths* challenge us to answer the question of whether we're on the road to life or death. The *two trees* challenge us to answer the question of whether we're listening to spiritual teachers who produce good fruit or bad fruit. The *two followers* challenge us to answer the question of whether we're true followers or false followers of Christ. And the *two houses* challenge us to answer the question of whether our eternal lives are built on a solid foundation or a sandy foundation.

Only one path and one gate leads to eternal life: the narrow one, chosen by few. Only one kind of teacher should be followed: the one whose preaching and practice square with Scripture. Only one kind of person is a true follower: the one whose faith in Jesus Christ is proved through obedience to His Word. Only one kind of person can have the

211

assurance of eternal life: the one whose faith in Jesus Christ can withstand the judgment of God.

The choice is yours. You can walk the wide path and enter the wide gate; you can eat the rotten fruit from false teachers; you can claim to know Jesus but disobey Him; you can build your spiritual house on the shifting sands by believing in anything but Jesus. But if you do, you face an eternity of death, fire, regret, and destruction.

Or you can walk the narrow path and enter the narrow gate; you can eat the good fruit from true teachers; you can claim to know Jesus and obey Him; you can build your spiritual house on bedrock by believing in Jesus and doing what He commands. If you do, you face an eternity of life, joy, assurance, and stability.

Heaven and hell await your decision.

A CALL TO RADICAL RIGHTEOUSNESS

STANDING AT FIVE FEET, SIX INCHES TALL, the French emperor Napoleon Bonaparte had an ego far bigger than his diminutive stature. Though not easily impressed by others, Bonaparte never failed to impress himself. On the morning of the decisive battle with the British at Waterloo, while eating breakfast with his generals, Bonaparte said, "I tell you, Wellington is a bad general, and the English are poor troops, and this will be a mere breakfast for us."[1] However, as history proved, Wellington had Bonaparte for lunch.

Though General Wellington didn't impress Bonaparte, the one person who did impress him was Jesus. During his exile on the island of Elba, Bonaparte reportedly said, "Everything in Christ astonishes me. His spirit overawes me, and his will confounds me. Between him and whoever else in the world, there is no possible term of comparison. He is truly a being by himself."[2]

That's the same reaction those who heard Jesus's teaching on the hillside had. Matthew recorded their response: "When Jesus had finished these words, the crowds were amazed at His teaching; for He was teaching them as one having authority, and not as their scribes" (7:28–29).

What made Jesus's authority remarkable was that He and His teaching were revolutionary. In one short sermon—one that takes fewer than eighteen minutes to read out loud—He described the *character* required of citizens who enter God's kingdom (5:1–12), the *calling* they should follow (5:13–16), the *conduct* they should demonstrate (5:17–7:12), and the *choices* and *commitments* they should make (7:13–27).[3]

> Never had the people heard their teachers challenge them to a life of radical righteousness as Jesus did (5:20).
>
> Never had any teacher claimed to speak on his own authority as Jesus did (vv. 22, 28, 32, 34, 39, 44).
>
> Never had any teacher claimed his words were equal to the Word of God as Jesus did (7:24, 26).
>
> Never had any teacher claimed to fulfill God's Word as Jesus did (5:17).
>
> Never had any teacher claimed to be the judge between those who entered and those who didn't enter the kingdom of God as Jesus did (7:21, 23).
>
> And never had any teacher taught with such authority as Jesus did, which is why the people were dumbfounded after He spoke (vv. 28–29).

If we looked through the rest of Matthew's Gospel, we'd see that many who listened to Jesus that day refused to take up His call to radical righteousness. They followed Him from town to town, hoping to get something from Him—a meal or a miracle—and they'd come out to listen to another rousing talk and be entertained by His stories, but to take Him seriously and commit their lives to what He was saying was just too revolutionary for them. However, others did take Him at His word and answered the call. They found their lives turned right side up, with a new meaning and a new mission.

But that was then. This is now. As Jesus did throughout His sermon, I've tried to do throughout this book: to challenge you to follow Him on the road of radical righteousness, to be counted among the ones who view and live life differently. Warning: if you choose to follow Jesus, you might be labeled a revolutionary, just as He was (and is). But the righteousness Jesus calls us to *is* radical.

Jesus never forced anyone to follow Him, and I certainly don't have the power to do so either. Jesus simply issued a call and left the final decision in the hands of those who heard.

That same decision is now yours to make. After spending time with Jesus—studying His teaching and considering its potential impact on your life—are you ready to answer His call to radical righteousness? Only your life and your eternal destiny hang in the balance.

NOTES

18 Minutes That Will Change Your Life

1. J. Dwight Pentecost agrees with this conclusion, writing, "The disciples, then, were not only the Twelve but the multitudes who had assembled to hear Him teach." See J. Dwight Pentecost, *The Words and Works of Jesus Christ: A Study of the Life of Christ* (Grand Rapids: Zondervan, 1981), 171.

Chapter 1 Straight Talk about Your Happiness

1. L. Frank Baum, *The Wonderful Wizard of Oz*, 100th anniversary edition (New York: HarperCollins, 2000), 60–61.

2. Max Lucado, *The Applause of Heaven* (Nashville: Thomas Nelson, 2013).

3. Luke's version of the Sermon on the Mount also includes the Beatitudes (Luke 6:20–26), though he only lists four groups: the poor in spirit, those who hunger and thirst for righteousness, those who weep, and those who are persecuted. For a comprehensive comparison and contrast of the Beatitudes between the two Gospels, see R. T. France, *The Gospel of Matthew*, The New International Commentary of the New Testament (Grand Rapids: Eerdmans, 2007), 162–63.

4. G. K. Chesterton, *The Paradoxes of Mr. Pond* (Cornwall: House of Stratus, 2008), 41.

5. Dallas Willard, *The Divine Conspiracy: Rediscovering Our Hidden Life in God* (San Francisco: HarperSanFrancisco, 1998), 100.

6. As quoted in John Moody, "Review of the Financial Markets," *Moody's Magazine* 13 (January–June 1912): 403.

7. C. S. Lewis, *The Lion, the Witch and the Wardrobe*, in *The Complete Chronicles of Narnia* (New York: HarperCollins, 1998), 99.

8. Derrick G. Jeter, "Wretched Are the Angry, Blessed Are the Meek and Makers of Peace," sermon, Coffee House Fellowship, Stonebriar Community Church, Frisco, Texas, May 23, 2010.

9. As quoted in William Barclay, *The Gospel of Matthew*, vol. 1, The New Daily Study Bible (Louisville: Westminster John Knox Press, 2017), 121.

10. R. Kent Hughes, *The Sermon on the Mount: The Message of the Kingdom*, Preaching the Word (Wheaton: Crossway, 2001), 65.

Chapter 2 Straight Talk about Your Faith

1. As quoted in John C. Maxwell, *Developing the Leader within You* (Nashville: Thomas Nelson, 1993), 103.

2. Hughes, *Sermon on the Mount*, 82.

3. Barclay, *Gospel of Matthew*, 137.

4. See Mark Kurlansky, *Salt: A World History* (New York: Penguin, 2002).

5. I expand more on this idea of delaying the decay in our culture in my book *Twilight's Last Gleaming: How America's Last Days Can Be Your Best Days* (Nashville: Worthy, 2012).

6. Barclay, *Gospel of Matthew*, 137, 141.

7. Charles R. Swindoll, *Simple Faith: Discovering What Really Matters* (Nashville: W Publishing Group, 2003), 57.

8. See Matthew 7:12; 11:13; 22:40; Luke 16:16; John 1:45; Acts 13:15; 28:23; Romans 3:21.

9. John R. W. Stott, *The Message of the Sermon on the Mount*, rev. ed., The Bible Speaks Today (Downers Grove, IL: InterVarsity, 2020), 42.

Chapter 3 Straight Talk about Your Relationships

1. Abraham Lincoln, "First Debate with Stephen A. Douglas at Ottawa, Illinois," August 21, 1858, in *The Collected Works of Abraham Lincoln*, vol. 3, ed. Roy P. Basler (New Brunswick: Rutgers University Press, 1953), 13.

2. On the twelve ways in which Jesus claimed equality to God, see Daniel Doriani, "The Deity of Christ in the Synoptic Gospels," *Journal of the Evangelical Theological Society* 37, no. 3 (September 1994): 339–40, as quoted in Thomas L. Constable, "Notes on Matthew, 2021 Edition," https://planobiblechapel.org/tcon/notes/pdf/matthew.pdf, 162.

3. *Twelve Angry Men*, directed by Sidney Lumet (1957; Hollywood: MGM, 2013), Blu-ray Disc.

4. See Robert Jeffress, *Invincible: Conquering the Mountains That Separate You from the Blessed Life* (Grand Rapids: Baker Books, 2021), 137–38.

5. As quoted in David McCullough, *John Adams* (New York: Simon & Schuster, 2001), 537.

6. As quoted in Stott, *Message of the Sermon on the Mount*, 64.

7. John Taylor, "Part of This Summer's Travels: Or News from Hell, Hull, and Halifax," in *Early Prose and Poetical Works* (London: Hamilton, Adams & Co., 1880), 303.

Chapter 4 Straight Talk about Your Sex Life

1. Dag Hammarskjöld, *Markings*, trans. Leif Sjöberg and W. H. Auden (New York: Knopf, 1965), 15.

2. Hammarskjöld, *Markings*, 15.

3. As quoted in Barclay, *Gospel of Matthew*, 170.

4. David Brooks, *The Second Mountain: The Quest for a Moral Life* (New York: Random House, 2019), 166.

5. Flavius Josephus, *Antiquity of the Jews*, 4.8.23, in *Josephus: Complete Works*, trans. William Whiston (Grand Rapids: Kregel, 1960), 99. During the time of Moses, only men could seek divorces since there was no provision for women to do so. However, by the time of Jesus, this provision had been changed (Mark 10:12).

6. The Pharisees questioned Jesus about divorce not so much to get His opinion on a controversy of the day but to trap Him in the hope He would contradict the law or His answer might land Him in political trouble with Herod Antipas.

7. I'm indebted to John R. W. Stott for the structure of this section and have adapted his observations. See Stott, *Message of the Sermon on the Mount*, 74–76.

8. For a more detailed treatment on what the Bible says about divorce and remarriage, see Robert Jeffress, *Grace Gone Wild!: Getting a Grip on God's Amazing Gift* (Colorado Springs: Waterbrook, 2005), 131–41.

9. *Peter Pan*, directed by Hamilton Luske, Clyde Geronimi, and Wilfred Jackson (Burbank, CA: Walt Disney Productions, 1953). Based on the novel by J. M. Barrie, *Peter and Wendy* (New York: Charles Scribner's Sons, 1911).

Chapter 5 Straight Talk about Your Adversaries

1. Ismail Kadare, *Broken April* (Chicago: New Amsterdam, 1982).

2. *The Untouchables*, directed by Brian De Palma (2007; Los Angles: Paramount Pictures, 1987). Blu-ray Disc.

3. The fourth illustration of radical righteousness, the command against swearing false oaths (Matt. 5:33–37), precedes these last two illustrations. In Jesus's day, people often promised to honor their vows by swearing on heaven, the earth, Jerusalem, or their own lives (vv. 34–36). But these oaths became an excuse for those who failed to honor their promises—they believed that since the vow wasn't made before God, they couldn't be held responsible to God. "Wrong," said Jesus. Instead of swearing oaths, Jesus said, "Let your statement be, 'Yes, yes' or 'No, no'; anything beyond these is of evil" (v. 37).

4. Thomas Jefferson et al., "Declaration of Independence, July 4, 1776, Philadelphia, Pennsylvania," in *The Constitution of the United States of America and Selected Writings of the Founding Fathers* (New York: Barnes & Noble, 2021), 108.

5. See Exodus 21:24; Leviticus 24:20; Deuteronomy 19:21.

6. As quoted in Barclay, *Gospel of Matthew*, 188.

7. Richard Langworth, ed., *Churchill by Himself: The Definitive Collection of Quotations* (New York: Public Affairs, 2011), 547.

8. Charles Haddon Spurgeon, *The Gospel of the Kingdom: A Popular Exposition of the Gospel according to Matthew* (London: Passmore and Alabaster, 1893), 30.

9. Corrie ten Boom, "Guideposts Classics: Corrie ten Boom on Forgiveness," *Guideposts*, November 1972, https://www.guideposts.org/better-living/positive-living/guideposts-classics-corrie-ten-boom-on-forgiveness.

10. Booker T. Washington, *Up from Slavery* (1901; Mineola, NY: Dover, 1995), 80.

11. As quoted in Swindoll, *Simple Faith*, 116.

Chapter 6 Straight Talk about Your Church

1. Ambrose Bierce, *The Devil's Dictionary* (New York: Barnes & Noble, 2007), 93.

2. The letter we know as 1 Corinthians is really Paul's second letter to this congregation. He wrote an earlier letter, which didn't survive (1 Cor. 5:9–11), prompting an additional letter—1 Corinthians. Paul then wrote a "severe" or "sorrowful" letter to the church at Corinth, which has also been lost to history (2 Cor. 2:3–4). The letter we know as 2 Corinthians, then, is actually Paul's fourth letter to the church.

3. Brennan Manning, voiceover on dc Talk, "What If I Stumble?" *Jesus Freak* (ForeFront/Virgin, 1995), compact disc. See also Ben Simpson, "The Ragamuffin Legacy," *Relevant*, April 16, 2013, https://www.relevantmagazine.com/faith/ragamuffin-legacy/.

4. Stott, *Message of the Sermon on the Mount*, 106–7.

5. Tobit 12:8–9, as quoted in Barclay, *Gospel of Matthew*, 216.

6. See, for example, Deuteronomy 15:11; Psalm 41:1; Proverbs 19:17.

7. See Ralph Gower, *The New Manners and Customs of Bible Times* (Chicago: Moody, 1987), 305, 306.

8. Jesus probably wasn't thinking of the metal, horn-shaped collection receptacles in the temple, though later in His ministry, He praised the widow who gave two mites (pennies) and didn't praise others who gave more (Luke 21:1–4). It could be that one reason she received praise from the Lord is not only because she gave out of her poverty while they gave out of their plenty but also because she quietly placed her two copper coins into the trumpet-like receptacles while the others threw in their heavier coins, which was a way of "sounding the trumpet" and drawing attention to their generosity.

9. As quoted in Constable, "Notes on Matthew," 184.

10. Spurgeon, *The Gospel of the Kingdom*, 32.

11. As quoted in Constable, "Notes on Matthew," 185, emphasis in original.

12. C. S. Lewis, *The Weight of Glory and Other Addresses* (San Francisco: HarperSanFrancisco, 2001), 26–27.

13. A. W. Tozer, *Born After Midnight* (Harrisburg, PA: Christian Publications, 1959), 107.

Chapter 7 Straight Talk about Your Prayer Life

1. Max Lucado, *Outlive Your Life: You Were Made to Make a Difference* (Nashville: Thomas Nelson, 2010), 157.

2. Karl Barth, as quoted in Philip Yancey, *Prayer: Does It Make Any Difference?* (Grand Rapids: Zondervan, 2006), 118.

3. We won't focus on hypocritical fasting in this book, but there are many great resources that address it. See, for example, Swindoll, *Simple Faith*; and D. A. Carson, *Jesus's Sermon on the Mount and His Confrontation with the World: A Study of Matthew 5–10* (Grand Rapids: Baker Books, 2018).

4. Barclay, *Gospel of Matthew*, 226, emphasis added.

5. As quoted in Constable, "Notes on Matthew," 187.

6. John Calvin, *Harmony of the Evangelists: Matthew, Mark, and Luke*, vol. 1, trans. William Pringle (Edinburgh: The Edinburgh Printing Co., 1845), 313.

7. Lucado, *Outlive Your Life*, 158–59.

8. As quoted in Stott, *Message of the Sermon on the Mount*, 113.

9. I'm indebted to my colleague Derrick G. Jeter for the wording of much of the material here, adapted from his "The Principles of Prayer" sermon at Coffee House Fellowship, Stonebriar Community Church, Frisco, Texas, June 1, 2015.

10. Hughes, *Sermon on the Mount*, 181.

11. Thomas Fuller, as quoted in Martin H. Manser, comp., *The Westminster Collection of Christian Quotations* (Louisville: Westminster John Knox Press, 2001), 113.

12. Jerry Sittser, *A Grace Disguised: How the Soul Grows through Loss* (Grand Rapids: Zondervan, 2004), 66.

13. This doxology probably didn't appear in Matthew's original Gospel, as penned by him, but was added later.

Chapter 8 Straight Talk about Your Money

1. The story of Elizabeth Johnson Williams is adapted from Emily Jones Shelton, "Lizzie E. Johnson: A Cattle Queen of Texas," *The Southwestern Historical Quarterly* 50, no. 3 (January 1947): 349–66.

2. Darrell L. Bock, *Jesus According to Scripture: Restoring the Portrait from the Gospels* (Grand Rapids: Baker Academic, 2003), 142.

3. The scientific name of the snail is *Bolinus brandaris*. See Colin Schulz, "In Ancient Rome, Purple was Made from Snails," *Smithsonian Magazine*, October 10, 2013, https://www.smithsonianmag.com/smart-news/in-ancient-rome-purple-dye-was-made-from-snails-1239931/; see also "Ancient Color: Creating Purple," University of Michigan, accessed January 14, 2022, https://exhibitions.kelsey.lsa.umich.edu/ancient-color/purple.php. Lydia, in the book of Acts, was "a seller of purple fabrics" (16:14).

4. See also Job 1:21.

5. As quoted in R. Kent Hughes, *To Guard the Deposit: 1 & 2 Timothy and Titus*, Preaching the Word (Wheaton: Crossway, 2000), 148, emphasis in original.

6. Andrew Carnegie, *The Gospel of Wealth: Two Essays by Andrew Carnegie* (Washington, DC: The Trinity Forum, 2005), 32.

7. Warren W. Wiersbe, *The Wiersbe Bible Commentary: The Complete New Testament in One Volume* (Colorado Springs: David C. Cook, 2007), 24, emphasis in original.

8. In some contexts, *haplous* can also mean "generous."

9. Lucius Annaeus Seneca, *Seneca's Morals by Way of Abstract*, ed. Roger L'Estrange (Cleveland: A. B. & Co., 1855), 205.

10. Alonzo L. McDonald, foreword to Carnegie, *Gospel of Wealth*, 10.

11. For a longer treatment about anxiety and worry, see Jeffress, *Invincible*, chapter 3.

12. See G. Campbell Morgan, *The Gospel According to Matthew* (Eugene, OR: Wipf & Stock, 1929), 67–68.

13. As quoted in Corrie ten Boom, *Clippings from My Notebook* (Nashville: Thomas Nelson, 1982), 33.

Chapter 9 Straight Talk about Your Needs

1. Carson, *Jesus's Sermon on the Mount*, 143–44.

2. Derrick G. Jeter, "The Practice and Purpose of Prayer," sermon at Coffee House Fellowship, Stonebriar Community Church, Frisco, Texas, June 7, 2015.

3. See Henry W. Holloman, "Sanctification: Rediscovering the Transforming Power of Sanctification," in *Understanding Christian Theology*, ed. Charles R. Swindoll and Roy B. Zuck (Nashville: Thomas Nelson, 2003), 1035–39.

4. Becky Freeman, "Attention, Children: The Bathroom Door Is Closed!," in Ann Spangler with Shari MacDonald, *Help, I Can't Stop Laughing!: A Nonstop Collection of Life's Funnies Stories* (Grand Rapids: Zondervan, 2006), 148.

5. As quoted in John Eldredge, *The Journey of Desire: Searching for the Life We've Only Dreamed Of* (Nashville: Thomas Nelson, 2000), 60.

6. William Barclay notes that the "snake" Jesus refers to was really an eel, which was forbidden to be eaten according to Jewish dietary laws (Lev. 11:12). See *Gospel of Matthew*, 312–13. In Luke's version, the bread is replaced with an egg, and the stone is replaced with a scorpion: "If [the father] is asked for an egg, he will not give [his son] a scorpion, will he?" (Luke 11:12); Barclay also notes, "there is a pale kind of scorpion, which, when folded up [tail and claws folded in], would look exactly like an egg."

7. Peter Kreeft, *Three Philosophies of Life* (San Francisco: Ignatius, 1989), 95.

8. Barclay, *Gospel of Matthew*, 314–15.

9. The recurrence of "the Law and the Prophets" takes us back to Matthew 5:17 and forms an *inclusio*—a bookend—indicating that everything between these verses is essentially an exposition of the Old Testament revelation.

10. The title "Golden Rule" traditionally comes from Roman emperor Alexander Severus, who ruled some two hundred years after Christ (AD 222–35). He wasn't a believer, but he was so taken with Jesus's statement in Matthew 7:12 that he had it engraved in gold on the wall of his bedchamber. See France, *Gospel of Matthew*, 284.

11. For negative examples, see Barclay, *Gospel of Matthew*, 315–17.

12. Søren Kierkegaard, *Upbuilding Discourses in Various Spirits*, trans. Howard V. and Edna H. Hong (Princeton: Princeton University Press, 1993), 22.

13. As quoted in James Boswell, *The Life of Samuel Johnson* (New York: Everyman's Library, 1992), 123.

Chapter 10 Straight Talk about Your Eternal Destiny

1. Peggy Noonan, *The Time of Our Lives: Collected Writings* (New York: Twelve, 2015), 302–3.

2. Robert Frost, "The Road Not Taken," in *Poems* (New York: Everyman's Library, 1997), 136.

3. For more about Jesus as the only way to heaven, see Robert Jeffress, *Not All Roads Lead to Heaven: Sharing an Exclusive Jesus in an Inclusive World* (Grand Rapids: Baker Books, 2016).

4. Jesus made the same point in Luke 13:22–30. There, He referred to Himself as "the narrow door," and said many would try to enter it but be unable to because they refuse to place faith in Christ, and by the time they come to an understanding of who He is, it will be too late—the door will have been shut.

5. Scott Chambers, as quoted in Tony Cagala, "This Cartoonist's Job Is to Find the Funny," *The Coast News Group*, February 26, 2017, https://thecoastnews.com/this-cartoonists-job-is-to-find-the-funny. Scott Chambers's cartoon is viewable at Henry Kotula, "Cartoon—Unpleasant Truths vs Comforting Lies," *A Healthcare Leadership Blog*, September 20, 2017, https://henrykotula.com/2017/09/20/cartoon-unpleasant-truths -vs-comforting-lies/.

6. For more about false prophets, see Deut. 13; 18; Jer. 6:13–15; 8:8–12; Ezek. 13; 22:27; Zeph. 3:4.

7. As quoted in Swindoll, *Simple Faith*, 237.

8. Carson, *Jesus's Sermon on the Mount*, 173.

9. See also James 2:14–20.

A Call to Radical Righteousness

1. As quoted in Andrew Hilliard Atteridge, *The Bravest of the Brave: Michel Ney, Marshall of France, Duke of Elchingen, Prince of Moskwa: 1769–1815* (London: Methuen & Co., 1912), 323.

2. As quoted in Philip Yancey, *The Jesus I Never Knew* (Grand Rapids: Zondervan, 1995), 83.

3. Adapted from Constable, "Notes on Matthew," 226.

ABOUT THE AUTHOR

Dr. Robert Jeffress is senior pastor of the fourteen-thousand-member First Baptist Church, Dallas, Texas, and is a Fox News contributor. He is also an adjunct professor at Dallas Theological Seminary. He has made more than four thousand guest appearances on various radio and television programs and regularly appears on major mainstream media outlets such as Fox News channel's *Fox and Friends*, *Hannity*, *Fox News @ Night with Shannon Bream*, and *Justice with Judge Jeanine*, as well as ABC's *Good Morning America* and HBO's *Real Time with Bill Maher*.

Dr. Jeffress hosts a daily radio program, *Pathway to Victory*, that is heard nationwide on over one thousand stations in major markets such as Dallas–Fort Worth, New York City, Chicago, Los Angeles, Houston, Washington, DC, Philadelphia, San Francisco, Portland, and Seattle.

Dr. Jeffress also hosts a daily television program, *Pathway to Victory*, that can be seen Monday through Friday on the Trinity Broadcasting Network (TBN) and every Sunday on TBN, Daystar, and the TCT Network. *Pathway to Victory* also airs seven days a week on the Hillsong Channel. His television broadcast reaches 195 countries and is on 11,295 cable and satellite systems throughout the world.

Dr. Jeffress is the author of twenty-seven books, including *Perfect Ending*, *Not All Roads Lead to Heaven*, *A Place Called Heaven*, *Choosing the Extraordinary Life*, *Courageous*, *Praying for America*, and *Invincible*.

Dr. Jeffress led the congregation of First Baptist Dallas in the completion of a $135 million re-creation of its downtown campus. The project is the largest in modern church history and serves as a "spiritual oasis" covering six blocks of downtown Dallas.

Dr. Jeffress graduated with a DMin from Southwestern Baptist Theological Seminary, a ThM from Dallas Theological Seminary, and a BS from Baylor University. In May 2010, he was awarded a Doctor of Divinity degree from Dallas Baptist University. In June 2011, Dr. Jeffress received the Distinguished Alumnus of the Year award from Southwestern Baptist Theological Seminary.

Dr. Jeffress and his wife, Amy, have two daughters and three grandchildren.

Delve Deeper with the
18 Minutes with Jesus Study Guide

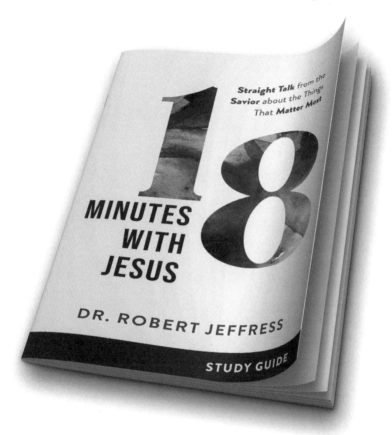

With thought-provoking questions and activities that help you delve even deeper into the Word of God, this study guide is the perfect tool to help you uncover truths that have the power to change your life.

Bring Eternity to Mind
EVERY DAY

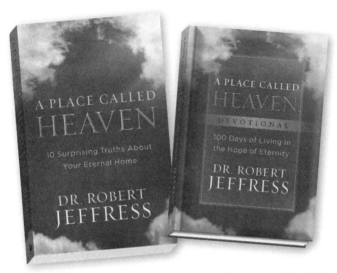

In his bestselling book *A Place Called Heaven*, Dr. Robert Jeffress opened the Scriptures to answer ten fascinating questions about heaven. Now he offers this devotional to help you think about heaven on a daily basis and put into practice the heavenly qualities of truth, honor, righteousness, purity, loveliness, character, excellence, and praise.

Colorfully illustrated and using simple concepts and language that children can understand, *A Place Called Heaven for Kids* gives children peace of mind about their lost loved ones as well as comforting, biblical pictures of their forever home.

Removing the Obstacles
That Stand between You and
GOD'S BEST

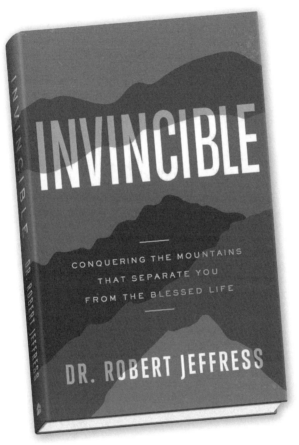

Dr. Robert Jeffress helps us identify and defeat the
mountains that threaten to keep us from experiencing
a blessed life. Offering biblical insight and practical tools,
Dr. Jeffress shows us how to put our faith in God,
rely on His power, and pray according to His will that
He will enable us to move the mountains in our lives.

A Clarion Call for You to Boldly
LIVE OUT YOUR FAITH

Just as survivalists use strategies to overcome threatening situations, *Courageous* explains ten biblical strategies for surviving—and thriving—in a world that is hostile to our faith. If you've felt your faith is under attack, or you're struggling with the temptation to follow the crowd despite biblical teaching to the contrary, *Courageous* will provide fresh fire and new hope.

Your Road Map to a Life of
ETERNAL IMPACT

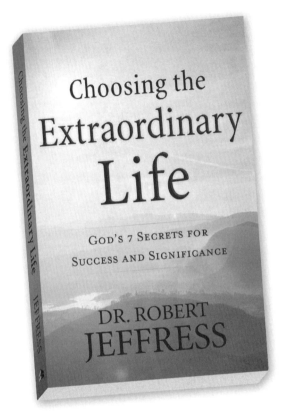

In this inspiring and motivating book, Dr. Jeffress reveals seven secrets from Elijah that result in a life marked by significance, satisfaction, and success, including

- · discovering your unique purpose in life
- · waiting on God's timing
- · learning how to handle bad days
- · and more

For anyone who wonders if there's more to life, God's Word reveals seven secrets for experiencing a truly extraordinary life.

Share the ONE TRUE WAY
of Salvation with Those in Your Life

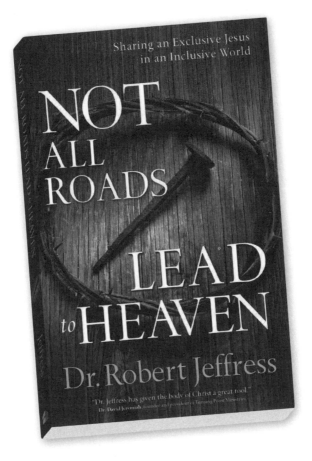

If you want to confidently and compassionately share the one true way of salvation with those in your life, or if you simply need to restore your confidence in the gospel message, this is the book for you.

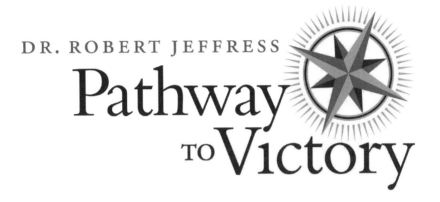

DR. ROBERT JEFFRESS

Pathway TO Victory

To find more information about Pathway to Victory's radio and television programs, to check out their online store, or to learn more about Dr. Jeffress, head to

WWW.PTV.ORG.